The Body Spiritual

A comparison of the physical and spiritual body

The Body Spiritual

A comparison of the physical and spiritual body

Victoria M. Moots, D.O.

TRILOGY

The Body Spiritual

Trilogy Christian Publishers A Wholly Owned Subsidiary of Trinity Broadcasting Network

2442 Michelle Drive Tustin, CA 92780

Manufactured in the United States of America

10 9 8 7 6 5 4 3 2 1

Library of Congress Cataloging-in-Publication Data is available.

ISBN: 978-1-64773-344-5

E-ISBN: 978-1-64773-345-2

ACKNOWLEDGMENTS

I would like to thank the many people (family members, patients, and friends) who encouraged me to publish a book of my medical sermons. A special thanks goes to Christy Rogers for her many hours of typing and for using her computer skills, which I lacked, in order to make it possible. Since "tribulation worketh patience," I know that God will bless her with an extra serving of patience for enduring the many tribulations that I gave her through the multiple revisions and corrections that I handed to her before we finally finished our project. But I must also thank God for His inspiration to write and His enabling, for without Him I could do nothing.

CONTENTS

INTRODUCTION

The content of this book is a melding of two distinct but inseparable disciplines of study: medicine and the Bible. The physical and the spiritual realms have been knit together.

As both a minister and a physician, I have been inspired by the fact that most people in the Bible sought out Jesus to meet their physical needs, but He also ministered to their spirits in order that they might be healed body, soul, and spirit. The apostle Paul compared the physical body to the spiritual body of Christ in chapter 12 of his letter to the Corinthians, as well as in Ephesians 4:15–16.

As I began to practice medicine and continued to study the Bible for my sermons, the Holy Spirit impressed on me that the various functions of the body and many common diseases have a spiritual correlation. At that point I began to give sermons that were basically medical parables that illustrated spiritual lessons. Such physical illustrations made it easier for people to understand the Bible.

This book is a compilation of some of those sermons that have been given over the past thirty-two years at camp meetings, church fellowship meetings, women's retreats, and Bible conferences, as well as in our own church. The subjects cover a variety of common topics, and they vary in length and complexity. Hopefully, they will appeal to readers of different ages and spiritual maturity and backgrounds.

Each topic was inspired by an encounter with an actual patient in my practice or from my own personal experience. These sermons are intended to provide both practical medical information as well as spiritual truth. Each is complete in itself and can be studied in more depth through the Scripture references provided, in a Bible study group, or during your own devotional time.

SCARS

Have you ever had a scar? Not long after birth we begin to accumulate scars, not just physical but emotional scars. I am going to discuss how scars are formed in the natural and apply that to our emotional scars, examining what they mean to us and why scars are necessary.

You may wonder why scars are necessary and why God couldn't make our wounds heal without scars. Wouldn't that be nice? But scars are a necessary part of the wound healing process. You may also wonder, *Why were there scars in Jesus' body? Why wasn't His body healed completely when He was raised from the dead?* We are going to look at the answer to these questions.

Scars are part of the natural healing process; they appear in all sizes: long, short, wide, and narrow, and they all tell a story. They tell a story of something that happened in the past, whether it was an injury or a surgery. They have a personal meaning to us. Also, bodies are identified by scars, tattoos, and other markings that are found by the coroner. As a doctor I can find out on a physical exam what kind of surgeries you have had, even if you have forgotten. I see a scar, and I ask, "What was this from?" Sometimes as you are telling me, you may become a little bit emotional because of the circumstances associated with the scar.

Scars are important physically and spiritually. Jesus was identified after His resurrection and will be identified in the future by His scars. In John 20:19–29, we read the account of when Jesus appeared to His disciples behind closed doors. He showed them His hands and His side, and they believed. But one of the disciples, Thomas, who wasn't there, stated that he would not believe unless he saw for himself and was able to put his finger into the print of the nails and thrust his hand into the wound in Jesus' side. We all know where the scar came from in His side: It was where the soldier thrust the spear into His heart to be sure He was dead. (I am going to talk a little more about what that scar meant later.) Thomas wanted to see the physical evidence that Jesus had been raised from the dead, so Jesus did appear to him later and invite him to examine those scars, and he believed.

Zechariah 13:6 states, "And one shall say unto him, What are these wounds in thine hands? Then he shall answer, Those with which I was wounded in the house of my friends." So, we see that Jesus' scars were His identification. Also, Zechariah 12:10 says, "...they shall look upon me whom they have pierced...."

As stated previously, scars are a reminder of an injury or surgery. They tell a story, and they can be a testimony of healing. Scars are not evidence of crucifixion, because you must be alive to make scars. Anyone else other than Jesus who was crucified did not have scars from that event, because they all died before any healing process could take place. Scars show healing, not just injury. Jesus' scars were evidence of His resurrection and healing.

Now let us examine the physical process of wound healing and scar formation to better understand their spiritual meaning. In the physical, this is a very complex process, but I am going to try to simplify it a little. It is actually called "regeneration," which means "replacement of destroyed tissue with new tissue."

Doesn't God do this spiritually for us also? The Scripture says that "if any man be in Christ, he is a new creature [creation]: old things are passed away; and all things are become new" (2 Cor. 5:17). So, when He regenerates us by virtue of the new birth, He replaces the old, destroyed tissue with new tissue. He doesn't just patch up our old, sinful life. He gives us a new life, a resurrection life; we are born again. This means the regeneration of our lives occurs when He takes away the old and replaces it with the new. Therefore, one of the purposes of scars in our lives is to create a new thing that is pleasing unto God.

Fibrosis is the formation of connective tissue, which we call scar tissue. That is what we see on the outside of our bodies as evidence of healing, but there is something very important going on inside of our bodies at the same time. Tissue injury, either through an accident or through surgery, causes bleeding that starts inflammatory events into motion. It happens spiritually and emotionally also. Sometimes we get angry and we become inflamed, but God uses that inflammation, for it is a necessary part of wound healing, both natural and spiritual.

Special cells, called mast cells and macrophages, release inflammatory chemicals that cause the capillaries (small blood vessels) to dilate (open up) and become permeable (or leaky). This allows white cells and plasma, which is rich in clotting proteins and antibodies, to seep into the injured areas. This happens very quickly, forming a clot to stop the bleeding, and it holds the wound edges together, sealing it off from bacteria. Then the outer part of the clot hardens and forms a scab. That's nature's "Band-Aid," which helps to protect the wound. Dead cells and other debris in the wound are eaten up by the macrophages (like Pac-Man).

In the spiritual sense, the Holy Spirit cleans up our emotional wounds in much the same way doing a hidden, inner work to rid us of the harmful debris that Satan and the world throw at us to try to destroy us. This is taking place underneath, below the scab, not on the outside. People sometimes try to add insult to injury by the things they say and the things they do to us, but on the inside the Holy Spirit is working in us to cleanse and heal us.

While the inflammatory process of wound healing is going on, the first phase of tissue repair, called "organization," begins. God is well organized. He does all things decently and in order, according to His plan for our lives, according to His schedule. Sometimes we get a little impatient and start picking at the scab. We say, "Okay, I want to see if there is any new skin under there." So, we pull the scab off, and subsequently the process of healing takes longer. We do the same thing spiritually, but God is patient. He continues to work with us, and the process of healing goes on. As a result, we may get a minor infection in there because we have "messed with it," and the scar may become a little bigger. But God works all things together for our good; the bigger the scar, the bigger the testimony can be. Even when we mess things up, God continues to work on the inside.

Next, granulation tissue forms, containing new blood vessels (capillaries) and fibroblasts, which grow into the wound to bridge the gap where the tissue has been split apart. The fibroblasts are somewhat elastic and actually pull the edges of the wound together to aid in the healing. How does this apply to us spiritually? In the same manner, God is working in us to help pull our broken lives and hearts back together. As we continue to cling to Him, it helps the healing process. The macrophages (the Pac-Man cells) begin to dissolve the old blood clot, which was necessary in the first place to stop the bleeding. Every part of the healing process is necessary. We can't leave any of the steps out. Everything that God does in our lives to help us heal from emotional scars is necessary, even the inflammatory phase, when we get angry with God. But God uses that inflammation for healing.

At the same time, the outer layer of skin (the epithelium) begins to regenerate, growing under the scab. Collagen fibers are laid down, and granulation tissue forms a fibrous patch that we call a scar. That is the permanent part of the healing process that stays there to hold the wound edges together. The scab needs to stay on until it begins to loosen around the edges and fall off. We need to leave our hands off physically and spiritually while God is doing the healing. The Holy Spirit is not only working in us, but He is also working in the other people, the ones who have hurt or injured us in some way, healing the inflammation.

We have all seen signs of inflammation: a little swelling and redness around the wound that is usually gone in a few days and does not indicate infection. If it is getting worse, then it could mean an infection is taking place. In the natural body, doctors usually sew the wound edges together to speed up healing and decrease the amount of scar tissue needed to seal the wound, but there will always be a scar.

When we have been offended, when we have been hurt, we need to go to the Lord, the Great Physician. He can decrease the size of the emotional scar we will have if we turn it over to Him early in the process. He can heal us if we turn it over to Him later, too, but we will have a bigger scar.

The amount of scar tissue formed depends on how deep and how wide the wound is. That means something to us spiritually also. Ephesians 3:18–19 tells us of the breadth and length and depth and height of the love of God, which passes knowledge. What does that mean to us? It means that no matter how deep or how wide our emotional scar is, His love can go deeper and wider than anything we have ever experienced. Why? Because Jesus experienced all our emotions. He became a man; He became like us. He suffered emotional wounds, His friends turned against Him, He was betrayed, He experienced grief, His earthly father died, He thirsted, He hungered, He was tired. There is nothing that we have experienced that Jesus hasn't already experienced for us. And so, His love is deeper, higher, and wider than our wounds. It passes our knowledge to understand that; we just need to experience it. How do we comprehend it, then, if it passes knowledge? We lay hold of it by experience, and then we *know* how great His love is. Whatever emotional need we have, don't think that He can't heal it. His love goes deeper and wider, and then He draws us close to Him, just like the fibroblasts do, to bring about the healing.

So, scars are necessary. We need to not pick at the scab, nor get impatient; just give the Lord time to work in our lives, keeping our hands off both physically and spiritually, allowing Him to do the healing.

The scars of Jesus tell a story of love and obedience to the will of His Father. He could have avoided them. But what did He pray in the garden? "...not my will, but thine, be done" (Luke 22:42). He said in Hebrews 10:7: "...I come to do thy will, O God". So, He went through the process of obtaining those scars because of His love for us. The scars in His hands will be seen by the world. But He had another wound. The scar from the wound that pierced His heart was only seen by those who were close and intimate with Him. He was behind closed doors, because in order to expose that wound, He had to pull apart His clothing, to partially disrobe. Only those who were close to Him and familiar with Him were allowed to see and touch that wound.

In Philippians 3:10, we read that Paul desired to know Him in the fellowship of His suffering. He desired to be close and intimate with the Lord. He wanted to know Him in the power of His resurrection. The power of His resurrection was evidenced by the fact that He had scars in His hands and side. Paul said he wanted more than just evidence, he wanted to fellowship with Jesus' suffering, being made conformable to His death. He wanted to enter into the suffering that Jesus experienced, not just the physical suffering when the soldier took the spear and pierced into His heart. He wanted to understand the emotional pain that Jesus experienced when He hung there on the cross, the emotional pain of being made sin. He wanted to enter into that kind of suffering. The physical suffering, though very great, was only part of the suffering that Jesus experienced. The other part was that He had to be made sin for us, and He willingly did that. If we want to know Him like Paul did, then we will get behind closed doors and we will touch Him and commune with Him. Paul said in Galatians 6:17: "…I bear in my body the marks of the Lord Jesus." He gloried in the scars that he received as a result of preaching the cross, because it glorified Christ. He gloried in the cross; he didn't want to know anything except the cross.

We can glory in the scars that we have received after we have healed, as it glorifies Christ. It is Christ in us. God allows circumstances in our lives that sometimes hurt us and leave scars. As we yield to the healing process, the scars can become testimonies of the Christ-life in us, the resurrected life of Christ.

I have a friend who had been in prison. He was always afraid that people would bring it up to him, that they would keep picking off the scab and causing pain. I told him that he needed to turn it over to the Lord and turn it into a testimony. The next time someone said something, he needed to say, "I'm so glad you brought that up, because I want to tell you what the Lord did for me while I was in prison. If I hadn't gone to prison, I wouldn't have had healing for my soul." Then they would quit talking about it because they didn't want to hear his testimony. You can do the same thing whenever someone tries to bring up something in your face. You can, through the power of the Holy Spirit, turn that scar into a testimony. God doesn't remove the scars. They are there for a reason.

Did you know that Jesus had no scars before He was crucified? How can I say that? Only the risen Christ had scars. As the Lamb of God, He was without blemish or spot, so that means He had no scars; He was perfect. Exodus 12:5 tells us that the Passover lamb had to be without blemish or spot. And 1 Peter 1:18–19 reminds us that Christ was that perfect Lamb. He had no scars. He was slain as the Passover Lamb for our sin. That's where He obtained His scars. Now He will bear those scars for eternity. Why? As a reminder to us and to the world that our sins will not be remembered, and that we will not be forgotten. Those scars are His for eternity.

Will our scars be present for eternity as well? I will answer that question later. So why are those scars in His hands now? In Isaiah 49:16, it says, "Behold, I have graven thee upon the palms of my hands…." What does that mean? The nail scars! When He looks at His hands, He sees us. He says, "That's Vicky; I died for her." When He looks at His hands, He sees each one of us individually. You can put your name in there. Those scars are His for eternity because of us.

In the natural, people don't want scars; they feel they mar their appearance. Surgeons and lawyers get rich from scars because of our vanity and pride. We desire the flesh to be perfect on the outside. Billions of dollars are spent on cosmetics and plastic surgery to cover up or try to remove scars. Are we doing the same thing spiritually, trying to cover up our scars?

The Scripture says that all who live godly in Christ Jesus will suffer persecution. That means we are going to have scars. Some will have physical scars for suffering for Jesus, some will have emotional scars, but we are going to have scars and we are going to have suffering. Why? So that we may reign with Him. Second Timothy 2:12 states: "If we suffer, we shall also reign with him...." As we yield to the Lord, we are going to accumulate scars, many scars. Those scars in our lives are marks of obedience to the will of God. We learn to know Him in the fellowship of His suffering. When our suffering gets to be too great for us, we can get behind closed doors with Jesus, get close and intimate with the Lord, and say to Him, "You have those scars because of me. Thank You, Lord. I thank You for the scars that I have received, because You are conforming me to Your image."

So, do we have enough scars in our lives that the world can identify the Christ-life in us? Are we covering those scars up; are we hiding them? Or are we allowing the Holy Spirit to use them as testimonies of healing? Don't hide your scars. The flesh is not perfect. He takes away the old and gives us the new; we are regenerated.

Someday our sin and suffering, scarred bodies will be healed. We are going to have glorified bodies, and I know we will not have scars in those bodies. Why? Because the Scripture says we are going to become His spotless bride. No scars! So, until then, let us allow our scars to become testimonies of what Christ has done in our lives, what He has done for us and in us.

SPIRITUAL HEART DISEASE

Of all diseases, heart disease is the number-one killer in the United States, surpassing even cancer. According to the CDC, almost 65,000 Americans die from it each year, and 20 percent of those are under the age of sixty-five. Approximately every forty seconds someone has a heart attack, and one out of five of these are silent attacks, with no warning signs. Heart disease is often overlooked in women because their symptoms are more subtle and often disguised as other problems such as indigestion, back pain, or unexplained fatigue, instead of chest pain. Symptoms of heart disease should not be ignored in the physical, nor should they be in the spiritual; they need to be evaluated.

The Bible has much to say about the heart, as it is also the number-one killer spiritually. Heart disease can lead to disability, not just death, because it could result in heart failure and a weakened state. We are going to see that this is also true spiritually.

The unregenerate heart of all mankind has been evaluated by God and found to be diseased. Jeremiah 17:9 states: "The heart is deceitful above all things, and desperately wicked." Therefore, we all need treatment for spiritual heart disease.

I am going to discuss the function of the heart and how heart disease can affect it, then apply this to us spiritually.

The heart is the pumping organ of the body that circulates the blood, which carries nutrients and oxygen to all the cells in the body. If it stops working, you die. If it does not work properly, you become weak and ill and can eventually develop congestive heart failure.

The heart has four chambers: two upper (the atria) and two lower (the ventricles). The atria receive the blood, and the ventricles do the pumping. The right side receives blood from the body and then sends it to the lungs to exchange carbon dioxide for oxygen. Then the blood flows to the left side, which is bigger as it must pump the blood to the whole body. The four chambers are not equal, but they are balanced and they must be synchronized to be effective. They are unequal in size and strength but equal in importance.

This is also true in the body of Christ, the church. We have been placed in the body according to God's choosing and given a ministry to perform. We are not equal in size, but we are of equal importance and must work together.

What would happen in the natural if the right ventricle became jealous of the left ventricle because it was bigger and thus decided to keep back some of the blood and not share it with the rest of the body—or if it refused to work with the left ventricle anymore? Even worse, suppose the right ventricle decided its job must not be very important so it just took the day off.

Now, perhaps the left ventricle thought it was better because it was bigger and its job was more important, so it decided to try to take on more work. As a result, since it is a muscle, it would just keep getting bigger. However, an enlarged heart is not good for the body. Either way, you would quickly go into heart failure.

This may sound absurd, but this sometimes happens in churches when members refuse to work together as a body and start comparing themselves to each other instead of to Christ.

A weakened heart is unable to pump enough of the blood it receives back to the rest of the body, so the blood backs up into the lungs, resulting in congestive heart failure. This condition was described by King Solomon in Ecclesiastes 12:6. In this chapter, he is describing things that happen to the physical body as it ages. Verse 6 states: "...the pitcher be broken at the fountain...." The fountain is symbolic of the heart, which makes the blood flow, and because pitchers are vessels that carry fluid, the pitcher would refer to the vessels that carry the blood. He is saying that the pitcher (the vessels) cannot carry the blood because there is a problem with the fountain (the heart), indicating heart failure.

One of the most common causes of heart failure is underlying coronary artery disease or atherosclerosis, which means hardening of the arteries. Cholesterol plaque builds up in the arteries of the heart due to a diet high in saturated fat and sugar. Inflammation in the walls of the vessels causes calcium to be deposited, and they become hardened. As the plaque continues to build up, the flow of the blood is decreased. If a clot forms in the narrowed artery, then it becomes completely blocked, resulting in a heart attack.

Risk factors that can cause this include improper diet, lack of exercise or limited activity, weight gain, diabetes, and smoking. Other risk factors such as age, sex, or genetics cannot be changed, so we must concentrate on the ones over which we have some control.

What about spiritually? God cannot flow through blocked vessels, so we need to guard against the things of the world that can cause hardness of the heart. In Mark 3:5, we see that Jesus was upset with the Pharisees and He "grieved for the hardness of their hearts," for they condemned Him for healing on the Sabbath. Legality had caused spiritual hardening of the arteries, and they became calcified, unmovable, and stiff. Hardened vessels cannot dilate or yield, so God was not able to flow through them. The Word of God will either soften or harden our hearts. Pharaoh's heart was likewise hardened when he rejected God's Word that was spoken through Moses.

Psalm 119:70 describes the hearts of those who are proud: "Their heart is as fat as grease." Pride causes our hearts to become hardened and resistant to hearing God's Word. Job stated as he was going through his trial: "He performeth the thing that is appointed for me" (Job 23:14). And in verse 16, "God maketh my heart soft." Job was yielding to the hand of God as He was purifying him, rather than becoming hardened.

We get fatty hearts in the natural by eating fat. Healthy oils are, however, beneficial. The Old Testament tells us what to do with fat; we do not need to wait for a doctor to tell us. Under the Mosaic law, all the fat from the animal sacrifices was to be burned on the altar, and none of it was to be eaten, for "all the fat is the LORD's" (Lev. 3:16). Fat is a good source of energy; it will burn and give off a hot fire. It produces energy but does not build you up; it just fills you up and fills you out. Fat is something our flesh lusts for. The more fat we eat, the more we want. This is not just a health precaution, for it has a spiritual meaning also. Fat speaks of fleshly zeal. We want to *do* something for God, but God has already done the work *for* us and wants to work *in* us. Our zeal needs to be given over to God so that He can work *through* us in order that *His* name will be glorified. Our works must be energized by God, not self. The zeal, the fat, belongs to God.

The apostle Paul, who was previously known as Saul before his conversion, had a zeal for God. He thought he was doing service to God when he persecuted the Christians. God saw his heart and turned that zeal around so he would preach the gospel instead of trying to destroy it. But he had to be humbled and come to the end of his own strength first. He had to give all of the fat to the Lord before God could use him. We should not eat the fat spiritually or physically if we want to avoid a hardened heart.

What should we do to find out if we have heart disease? First of all, if you are aware of any physical symptoms that are suspicious, you should seek medical attention as soon as possible. The psalmist, David, sought help from God when his heart began to trouble him spiritually. He recognized the symptoms, for he said, "My heart is sore pained within me" (Ps. 55:4); and he cried out "when my heart is overwhelmed: lead me to the rock that is higher than I" (Ps. 61:2). He went to the Great Physician and requested, "Search me, O God, and know my heart…" (Ps. 139:23). God knows the reason why our hearts are pained or troubled, and He wants to heal us. All we need to do is to call upon Him.

In the natural, to evaluate you, a cardiologist would likely do a stress test by putting you on a treadmill to see if there are any changes suspicious of coronary artery disease that would show up on the EKG tracing or on the nuclear scan. The treadmill, of course, would not *treat* the problem, only cause it to show up, for it only *tries* the heart.

God tries our heart also, as we read in 1 Chronicles 29:17: "I know also, my God, that thou triest the heart." The Law was given to show the wickedness in our hearts. But, just like the treadmill, it can only reveal the problem, not provide the remedy. However, God *did* provide the remedy through His Son, as we find in 1 John 1:7: "...the blood of Jesus Christ his Son cleanseth us from all sin."

If the stress test is abnormal, then you proceed to a cardiac catheterization. For this test, dye is put into the heart arteries to determine where the blockage is located. In order to have this test you must sign a consent form to give your permission for that procedure and possibly a balloon and stent to treat the problem if needed.

We need to seek God and give Him permission, as did David when he said, "Create in me a clean heart..." (Ps. 51:10). God desires to clean out our hearts. We are all God's chosen vessels after we accept Christ, and He wants to flow through us. We need to submit to Him to search out the problem and allow Him to remove anything that is blocking His will in our lives, things that may be hindering the flow of the Holy Spirit.

Do we really want the Lord to try our hearts and search out our secret faults? Sometimes we even have things that we have hidden from ourselves, but they come out of our mouth under stress, for "…out of the abundance of the heart the mouth speaketh" (Matt. 12:34). If anger is hidden in our heart, it will come out when we are tested. Do we have any hidden anger or unforgiveness toward someone in the past (or present)? We must be like David when he asked God in Psalm 19:12: "cleanse thou me from secret faults." It is only as we allow the Lord to examine our hearts and uncover the secrets that are hidden that He can heal us.

If a blockage is discovered during the heart catheterization, the cardiologist guides a small wire with a balloon through the narrowed opening and then inflates it. When the balloon is deployed there may be severe pain, but it is only momentary and it serves a purpose. The balloon must be expanded long enough and hard enough to crush the plaque and restore the flow, but the doctor knows when to stop.

This is true spiritually when we go through trials. We don't like the crushing because of the pain, but the end result is an open, clean vessel. Job went through a time of severe testing and a fiery trial, but he was purified as a result, and his end was better than his beginning. Paul was also a "chosen vessel" (Acts 9:15) that God desired to use, but God had to humble and crush him first. Paul said, concerning his trials, in 2 Corinthians 4:17: "our light affliction, which is but for a moment, worketh for us a far more exceeding and eternal weight of glory".

God knows, just like the cardiologist, how long to do the crushing or the chastening. He does this through His Word, other people, or circumstances so that we can become "a vessel unto honour" (2 Tim. 2:21), fit for the Master's use.

What can the cardiologist do if the blocked vessel cannot be opened because the blockage is too severe? The next step would be to refer the patient to a surgeon for a coronary artery bypass graft or "CABG." In order to do this, the surgeon must take a useable clean vessel from another part of the body and bypass the blocked vessel. The blocked unusable vessel is not removed, only bypassed, for after a period of time it may actually open up enough where blood can flow through it again.

This is the same thing that God sometimes has to do in the body of Christ when a vessel becomes defiled, obstructing the flow of the Holy Spirit, and is no longer capable of fulfilling their ministry in the church. That person is then bypassed until such time that their heart has been cleaned and useable again.

In the natural a bypass is quite a painful surgery from which to recover. Likewise, it hurts God to have to bypass an individual and use someone else in their place. Therefore, a bypass is always done as a last resort, both physically and spiritually. It is God's desire to keep us as vessels of honor, open and yielded, so He can flow through us in the place He has chosen for us.

What keeps us from yielding? Why does the plaque build up in the first place and cause blockage? Is there anything we can do to prevent it? Let me answer these questions by first discussing our options for the natural body. I have already addressed the fact that diet is important. We must avoid eating saturated animal fat, which is high in cholesterol, but our bodies need the healthy fat that is found in vegetable products, such as olive oil, coconut oil, and avocados. A diet high in sugar and processed carbohydrates can also be harmful because it raises triglycerides and insulin levels, causing fat to be deposited in the liver and other internal organs such as the heart. The processing of grains removes the fiber, an important part of the food that actually lowers cholesterol. A diet high in fiber is beneficial for the heart and health in general. We should limit packaged, processed foods and "fast foods" as much as possible to try to prevent atherosclerosis and the development of diabetes and weight gain. These foods are usually high in fat, salt, and sugar, causing us to actually crave them and want to eat more.

How does this apply to us spiritually? We are to feed upon the pure, unadulterated Word of God's grace, which is able to build us up and strengthen us. The so-called gospel that is being preached in many modern churches today has been highly processed and "fortified" with man's ideas and laden with sugar. Their version of the bread of life has no fiber or nutrients with which to sustain us, and instead it tastes and smells more like fried pastries. It attracts the crowds and pleases the flesh, but it is not able to provide any nourishment for the soul. We must feed upon the true Bread from heaven and the "sincere milk of the Word" of His grace, which is able to build us up, purify us, and strengthen us. The fat belongs to the Lord so that He can energize us with His power. Without the fat we will not become blocked vessels.

In addition to diet, exercise is an important factor for prevention. Walking is the easiest and safest for all ages and does not require special equipment. Just fifteen minutes a day can decrease your risk of a heart attack if that is all you are able to do, although thirty minutes would be ideal. It does not even need to be done all at one time. I have advised my patients with diabetes to walk for five to ten minutes after each meal to lower their blood sugar and to help protect their hearts. You could walk back and forth in the house if unable to go outside, even with a walker, from the living room to the kitchen (but not to the refrigerator!). You could also stand in front of the couch or chair and march in place during TV commercials in order to increase your activity level.

Bodily exercise profits us while in this life, but spiritual exercise is even more important. Paul instructed Timothy to "refuse profane and old wives' fables, and exercise thyself rather unto godliness. For bodily exercise profiteth little [for a little time]: but godliness is profitable...of the life that now is, and of that which is to come" (1 Tim. 4:7–8). We can do this by "walking in wisdom" (Col. 4:5) through heeding the Word of God and by "walking in the light" (1 John 1:7).

There is another form of spiritual exercise that none of us particularly enjoys, but it is extremely rewarding if we are faithful to endure it. This is prescribed for us by God in Hebrews 12:11: "no chastening...seemeth to be joyous, but grievous: nevertheless afterward it yieldeth the peaceable fruit of righteousness unto them which are exercised thereby." It is this kind of exercise that may be able to condition us enough so that we can "run, and not be weary" and "walk, and not faint" (Isa. 40:31) and be able to "run with patience the race that is set before us" (Heb. 12:1). This is God's desire for us, and it should also be our desire.

Psalm 102 is known as the "Rejection Psalm," and it expresses Christ's feelings prophetically as He was rejected by those to whom He came to minister. Verse 4 says, "My heart is smitten [under attack]." His heart was pained and broken for Israel and also for us. We, the vessels closest to Him that are blocked, are the ones causing His heart to ache because we do not yield to Him. When we become hardened and do not allow free flow of the blood, hindering the Holy Spirit, it not only affects the rest of the body, but it brings sorrow to the Lord. We must, therefore, be willing to let God purify our hearts and cleanse us from spiritual heart disease, while we continually feed upon His Word and, like David, cry out, "Let my heart be sound [healthy] in thy statutes [thy Word]" (Ps. 119:80). His Word is living and powerful and able to bring healing to our broken or hardened hearts.

CHRIST IN YOU:

A Comparison to Pregnancy

"To whom God would make known what is the riches of the glory of this mystery…which is Christ in you, the hope of glory" (Col. 1:27). How is this possible, that Christ, the very Son of God, can live inside and be a part of us? This is truly a great mystery. It was a very important subject to the apostle Paul, who also wrote in Gal. 2:20: "I am crucified with Christ: nevertheless I live; yet not I, but Christ liveth in me…." He further told the Galatians: "…I travail in birth again until Christ be formed in you" (Gal. 4:19). In order to better understand this spiritual truth, God has given us an example in the natural. Christ is formed in us in much the same way as a baby is formed and developed in a mother's womb.

A new life begins at the moment of conception, when the sperm unites with the egg. The woman's body spends two weeks preparing for conception. During this time, under hormonal influence, the egg is ripening and the inside of the uterus is being built up with a special lining, or "nest" of blood vessels in which the egg will implant and be nourished. Then ovulation occurs, which is the release of the egg from the ovary into the fallopian tube, where it can be fertilized by the sperm. In order for this to take place, the sperm must travel upstream, fighting against the contractions of the muscles in the walls of the tube that are working hard to propel the egg downward toward the uterus.

In addition to that obstacle, the egg has a barrier around it that must be broken down by enzymes in the head of one of the sperm cells, which attacks it at one point and dissolves it, thus opening a "door." As soon as one sperm enters the egg the "door" is closed so that no other sperm can enter. Chemical changes also occur on the surface of the egg which prevent the enzymes of any other sperm from dissolving it so that there can only be one father of each baby. The genetic material of the sperm and egg unite and the two become one being.

What does this mean to us spiritually? The angel Gabriel told Mary, a virgin, that she would conceive and bear a child, the Son of God, by the over shadowing of the Holy Ghost. He also informed Joseph that the child she conceived was "...of the Holy Ghost" (Matt. 1:20). Just as the life of Christ in Mary was conceived by the Holy Spirit, so it is in us.

The Holy Spirit is the one and only agent of the new birth. He was sent into this world by God the Father to reprove (convict and convince) the world of sin. John 16:8 states: "when he is come, he will reprove the world of sin...." He "overshadows" us in the same manner as He did Mary, moving in our hearts to break down any barriers that cause us to resist Him, that separate us from God, and He causes us to realize that we are sinners and need to be born again. The door is opened, and He is then able to enter our hearts so that new life begins, the life of Christ in us.

At the moment of conception, there is only one cell, yet all the genetic material is present (the provision has been made) that is necessary for the formation of a being who will bear the image of his or her earthly father. When we are first born again (conceived by the Holy Spirit), we do not yet manifest the characteristics of our heavenly Father, but the provision is there. Only as we mature spiritually will we begin to bear His image, "as we have borne the image of the earthy, we shall also bear the image of the heavenly" (1 Cor. 15:49). But all this takes time and patience, waiting for growth to occur.

In the natural, the egg travels from the fallopian tube into the uterus, where it implants and obtains nourishment. Likewise, in the spiritual we must become rooted and grounded in Him, in His love, and in His Word, in order to mature into the fullness of His image (Eph. 3:18–19).

A normal pregnancy lasts forty weeks from conception to birth. The number forty in Scripture speaks of a time of testing. For example, Israel spent forty years in the wilderness, Jesus had a forty-day period of testing in the wilderness prior to beginning His public ministry, and Noah experienced forty days and nights of rain at the time of the flood. The duration of pregnancy is divided into three periods of three months, called trimesters. The number three refers to the Trinity, the triune God.

The first trimester is the most difficult time for the woman, but it is also the most important for the development of the baby. The vital organs and nervous system, including the brain, are all being formed at this time, even though there is no evidence of growth on the outside. David exclaimed in Psalm 139:15: "...I was made in secret...."

The new life that is being formed grows in response to the nutrients provided through the placenta in the mother's uterus, yet the baby itself is totally separated from the mother's body by the placental barrier. The baby develops its own blood supply, and the blood of the mother does not mix with the blood of the baby. In fact, they may have two different blood types. This means that none of Jesus' blood came from His mother, Mary. The Christ life in us is *not* dependent on our life (blood) or our works, but it grows as we feed on the Word of our heavenly Father.

During the first trimester the mother experiences hormonal changes in her body that may cause her to become very nauseated. She knows that she needs proper rest and good nutrition, but she finds it difficult to eat the right things when even the smell of food causes nausea. At this point she may become discouraged, feeling that pregnancy isn't such a wonderful thing after all. But her doctor informs her that things will soon get better, so she must be patient. Although a new life is present and growing daily, no one can see it and she doesn't even feel it yet. It seems as if those around her just don't understand how she feels or why she is discouraged.

This is often true in the spiritual. A new Christian may face trials and tribulations at a time when they think that Jesus is supposed to make everything work out just right. Older Christians may feel that the new convert is not following Christ because they see no evidence of growth taking place. Newborn Christians need encouragement, not condemnation, from God's Word and His people, to let them know that these things will pass, and they can be victorious. They need to be taught to rest on God's promises and His provision instead of focusing on their feelings and failures. We are to "rest in the LORD, and wait patiently for him…" (Ps. 37:7).

Because of the rapid development of vital organs during the first trimester, the new life is vulnerable to the effects of anything the mother takes into her body, as these things could cause birth defects. Likewise, new Christians must be cautioned to guard against things that enter the spirit through their eyes and ears, which could hinder the development of the Christ-life within. We need to feed upon the "sincere milk" of the Word of God to nourish the new-creation life that is in us, enabling us to become more like Him (1 Pet. 2:2).

The second trimester heralds the time when the woman first experiences the baby's movements. This event is called "quickening," which means "being made alive." Of course, the baby has been alive for the past three months, but now its life becomes real to the mother for the first time. The baby has been kicking and squirming for a while, but the movements were too small to be felt before now. The mother still cannot see the baby, but she knows now without a doubt that it is alive.

As we grow spiritually, the Holy Spirit can make Christ just as real to us. Psalm 119:50 states: "…thy word hath quickened me [made me alive]." As we read and study the Word, the Holy Spirit makes the *provision* of "Christ in me" become real in our *experience*; then we begin to manifest the life of "Christ in us" to the world. Second Peter 3:18 instructs us to "grow in grace and in the knowledge of our Lord and Savior Jesus Christ.…" Even Jesus grew strong in spirit and in grace (Luke 2:40).

The baby's life is now beginning to affect the outward appearance and actions of the mother. Her walk, talk, and clothing begin to change. She no longer feels comfortable doing the same things or wearing the same clothes that she did before. She begins to talk more and more about the baby to everyone she knows and even to those she does not know. Everything else in her life becomes less important in comparison to the new life that is within her.

As Christians, the new life within us should also have an effect on our manner of life, our actions, appearance, and speech. In fact, it should be so obvious to those around us that Christ lives within that we would not need to wear a T-shirt that says "I am a Christian" any more than a pregnant woman needs a shirt that says, "I am pregnant."

By the third trimester, the baby is almost fully developed and *could* survive outside the womb, even though the lungs are not yet fully matured. The "finishing touches" are still needed. So it is in the spiritual realm: "speaking the truth in love, may grow up into him in *all things*..." (Eph. 4:15); "... unto a perfect [mature] man, unto the measure of the stature of the *fullness* of Christ" (Eph. 4:13).

As the "due date" approaches, the mother begins to make final preparations for the coming of her baby. She is truly and eagerly "expecting." She does not know the exact day nor the hour, but she is aware of changes in her body that signal the time is near. She may experience "Braxton Hicks" contractions during the last month, which are mild, intermittent muscular contractions of the uterus, thought to be a kind of "warming up" exercise for the final event of labor.

Doctors do not know what actually triggers the onset of true labor contractions, but they can tell by some physical changes found on examination when the time is close. Likewise, the Scripture tells us that no man knows the day nor hour of the Lord's coming, but when we see certain signs coming to pass, we can know that it is near (Matt. 24:32–36).

We can already feel the labor contractions, the increased pressures in the world around us, indicating that the time of His coming is fast approaching. The daily newscasts are filled with some of these signs, which should warn those who are not ready to get prepared. But they should also fill hearts with joy at the nearness of His return for His bride, for those who have been patiently "expecting."

In the physical birth process, shortly before a baby is born, the head drops into the pelvis, into the proper position to pass through the birth canal. This is called "becoming engaged." We must allow the "Christ in us" to become fully mature by the "…word of his grace, which is able to build you up…" (Acts 20:32), and become "engaged," for there is soon to be heard the shout of His coming, and the Lamb will take His bride. "He which testifieth these things saith, Surely I come quickly. Amen. Even so, come, Lord Jesus" (Rev. 22:20).

SPIRITUAL CANCER

Almost everyone's life has been touched by cancer, either through personal experience or through the diagnosis of a family member or loved one. There were more than 1.5 million new cases of cancer diagnosed in 2017 (not including skin cancer), and the number is increasing each year.

If a disease in the natural is that prevalent, then it must have an important spiritual lesson to teach us. The Bible doesn't contain the word *cancer*, but it does use a similar word with a similar meaning in Second Timothy 2:17. The word I'm referring to is *canker*, which actually means "gangrene," or something that devours and destroys the flesh. Verse 15 tells us to "study to shew thyself approved unto God, a workman that needeth not to be ashamed, rightly dividing the word of truth." This is our guard against spiritual cancer. If we know the truth and are grounded in the Word, we will not be led astray by error. What is cancer? In the natural, it is a disease caused by normal cells that have gone wild and are growing out of control. We need to understand what a normal cell is like in order to understand the abnormal cell. There are over 75 trillion cells in the human body. Each one is a living structure by itself more complex than the city of New York, but they all join together to form one body. Each cell has three basic parts (we are a trinity even at the cellular level, because we are created in His image). Each part represents a person in the Godhead.

An example in the natural that can be seen without a microscope is the egg. It has an outer shell, representing the cell membrane; the white represents the protoplasm; and the yolk represents the nucleus. The nucleus contains DNA (genetic material) that controls each cell and its relationship to the other cells and their growth. This is a type of God the Father, who is Ruler over all things.

The protoplasm (or cytoplasm) is the cellular material between the cell membrane and the nucleus. Its liquid is a complex mixture of nutrients that supports cell growth and organelles (little organs), such as the mitochondria and other structures that help provide the energy and do the manufacturing of proteins to maintain the life and growth of the cell. It represents Christ, who is our supply. Philippians 4:19 states: "My God shall supply all your need according to his riches in glory by Christ Jesus."

Lastly, the cell membrane is the outer envelope of the cell that holds everything in its proper place. It contains microscopic "gates," or channels, that regulate what enters and exits the cell, such as sodium, potassium, and calcium. This is necessary to maintain the electrical charge and the proper pH (acid-base balance) of the cell. It represents the work of the Holy Spirit in our lives.

We all began our lives as a single cell after fertilization took place. Then the DNA in the nucleus signaled for growth to occur, causing the cells to divide and multiply into many more cells. All cells started out identical and subsequently began the process of differentiation to form different body parts. All the cells in one body have the same DNA and work together, joining to form one body through the influence of the DNA in the nucleus. Can you see the correlation in the spiritual body?

In the cell membrane, surrounding each cell are factors that tell each cell that it is touching another cell. This is a feedback mechanism that helps to avoid one cell crowding out the other cells. The principle is called "contact inhibition." Through this factor each cell feels the presence and need of the other cells, thus preventing it from crowding out the other cells, allowing each cell to only grow at the rate it is supposed to grow, under the influence of the nucleus.

Cancer cells are normal cells that somehow become influenced by something else. Their growth is no longer controlled by the nucleus. They grow rapidly at their own rate, at their own desire, without any respect or concern for the other cells. They have lost their "contact inhibition," and they crowd out the other cells. They quickly use up their own nutrients and then begin to feed on the other surrounding cells.

Galatians 5:13–16 gives us an example in the spiritual body. Verse 13 states: "...use not liberty for an occasion to the flesh but by love serve one another [spiritual contact inhibition]." And verse 14 continues: "For all the law is fulfilled in one word, even in this; Thou shalt love thy neighbor [cell] as thyself." If we serve one another in love, then we will not crowd out or hinder one another's growth. Verse 15 says this: "But if ye bite and devour one another, take heed that ye be not consumed one of another." (That's what cancer cells do: They devour the other cells.) Verse 16 continues to instruct us: "...walk in the spirit, and ye shall not fulfill the lust of the flesh." The spirit gives us the spiritual "contact inhibition" needed. If we heed the control of the nucleus (our Head), we will serve one another in love. The desire of the flesh is to be "me first." Paul is not just talking about the carnal lusts of the flesh; he is talking about pride and the desire to get ahead of someone else even if it means pushing them out of the way.

In First Corinthians 1:10, we read, "Now I beseech you, brethren, by the name of our Lord Jesus Christ that ye all speak the same thing, and that there be no divisions among you...." We can all speak the same thing (speaking the truth in love) if we have the mind of Christ. The cancer cell loses its differentiation and becomes "undifferentiated" (having a different appearance under the microscope). It is disorganized and no longer looks like a normal cell, no longer recognizable. In verse 11 we read, "...there are contentions among you." These are divisions, separations in the body of Christ, in which the members are no longer speaking the same thing. This is spiritual cancer.

What has changed? The nucleus is no longer in control, and so the cell takes over and grows at its own rate, doing its own thing, devouring the other cells. A cancerous growth not only looks different under the microscope, but it feels different to the touch. It becomes hardened and unyielding,in addition to acting differently.

If a woman finds a lump in her breast that feels different than the rest of her breast tissue, she goes to a doctor for an examination. The doctor examines her and applies principles according to the standards of medicine. Through a physical exam, the doctor can tell if it feels soft like a normal cyst, or if it is a suspicious lump, in which case he would order more tests to confirm the diagnosis.

In First Corinthians 12:12, Paul tells us, "For as the body is one, and hath many members, and all the members of that one body, being many, are one body: so also is Christ." Verse 18 further tells us, "But now hath God set the members every one of them in the body, as it hath pleased him." Likewise, He created the physical body to function as a unit under the direction of the head, all members working together for the good of the body.

As a spiritual body, we need to let the nucleus (our Head) control our growth and differentiation as it pleases Him. We need to let each member grow at his or her own rate and fulfill his or her own place of ministry, giving the feeble members more time to grow. We are to help them, not devour them. First Corinthians 12:25 warns us, "That there should be no schism [cancer] in the body; [a schism is a division in the body, an unyielding; a hardness; a separation; a spiritual cancer], but that the members should have the same care one for another." Each cell is as important as the other.

What can we do to try to prevent cancer or to detect it early? Physicians teach patients to do self-exams, such as breast self-examination for women and testicular self-examination for men, to check for lumps or swelling. First Corinthians 11:28 advises us, "…let a man examine himself…." Have you checked yourself? Are you hard, unyielding? Do you have love or bitterness in your heart? Note that Paul says to examine *ourselves*, not each other. Don't examine each other for cancer, either physical or spiritual. Only two people should be examining your body—you and your doctor. Don't try examining your neighbor—it could get you in trouble! The same thing applies spiritually.

A cancer that is not curable is one that goes unnoticed or ignored. Watch for warning signs: unusual bleeding, blood in the urine or bowels, postmenopausal bleeding, or sores that bleed or will not heal. Then go see your doctor! *Do not delay!*

What are some of the potential causes or risk factors of cancer? Smoking or chewing tobacco is a major contributor to multiple types of cancer, including oral, esophageal, stomach, bladder, and lung cancer. This is both due to irritation and the toxic chemicals in tobacco. Also, toxic exposure to other chemicals, radiation, or overexposure to the sun (especially sunburns) can increase your risk of cancer. Spiritually this speaks of legality—constantly judging others or self-condemnation. The sunlight of God's Word shows us our sins, and then we are to cover ourselves with His righteousness. Romans 8:1 is our protection from God's judgment: "There is therefore now no condemnation to them which are in Christ Jesus...." This is our spiritual sunblock to avoid spiritual skin cancer, but we must apply it personally.

Improper nutrition can result in alteration of our body's immune system and cause us to be more susceptible to cancer. A diet that consists mainly of highly processed foods, high in sugar and hydrogenated fats, and lacking in fresh fruits and vegetables has been associated with an increased risk of diabetes and cancer. To be healthy spiritually we are to "...desire the sincere milk of the word..." (1 Pet. 2:2) and "...shun profane and vain babblings..." (2

Tim. 2:16). We must feed our souls with the nutritious Word of His grace daily and study to show ourselves approved unto God (2 Tim. 2:15).

But what is a doctor's next step after a newly discovered lump has been found and all the tests confirm that it is malignant? One of the hardest things I have ever had to do as a physician has been to tell a patient, "You have cancer." Before healing can begin, however, the truth must be told, not in a cold, uncaring way, but with love, compassion, and hope. Sometimes the truth hurts. But not to know the truth is even more painful. By "…speaking the truth in love…" (Eph. 4:15), we bring hope, not condemnation.

Neither spiritual nor physical cancer can be cured if you do not accept the diagnosis and submit to the treatment. Romans 12:10 gives us the cure for spiritual cancer: "Be kindly affectioned one to another with brotherly love; in honour preferring one another." Only by the love of God, which is shed abroad in our hearts by the Holy Ghost (Rom. 5:5), can this be possible. "Love worketh no ill to his neighbor…" (Rom. 13:10). Romans 15:1–2 tells us that we are not to please ourselves but we are to please our neighbor for his good to edification. That means we are to build up (to edify), not to crowd out or to devour our neighbor cell. Love is our "contact inhibition."

We do not have to let things enter into our souls that feed the flesh. Remember the cell membrane surrounding each cell represents the Holy Spirit in our lives and has gates or channels to control what enters or exits the cell. We must yield to the Holy Spirit and allow Him to control our emotions, desires, and actions in order to prevent spiritual cancer.

Let us examine ourselves to see if we have spiritual cancer and then go to the Great Physician for healing. Sometimes the treatment is not very pleasant. We don't like the cutting, the bitter medicine, or the trials, but we learn that all things work for our good, if we trust Him and yield to the Holy Spirit.

SPIRITUAL LUNG DISEASE

Breathing is an essential part of life; it has been ever since God breathed into Adam, the first man, the breath of life (Gen. 2:7). In the Greek, the word *pneuma* is used for both "breath" and "spirit." It is from this root word that we obtain the term *pneumonia* and other diseases related to the lung. It means "a current of air" or "a blast."

Acts 2:2–4 records the account of God breathing the breath of life, the Holy Spirit, into the church on the Day of Pentecost. Verse 2 states: "And suddenly there came a sound from heaven as of a rushing mighty wind [a blast]." Verse 4 continues: "And they were all filled with the Holy Ghost...." The church was brought to life in the same manner as when God breathed into Adam.

When a baby is born, it must take its first breath of air after living for nine months surrounded by water in the womb. A lusty cry is necessary to expand the lungs and force the fluid out. The doctor, or other birth attendant, quickly suctions out the nose and mouth as soon as the head is out so that nothing is obstructing the airway. It must be cleared to allow air to move in and out.

The natural process of breathing is divided into two parts: inspiration and expiration, or exhalation. Inspiration brings the oxygen into the body, to the lungs, to be delivered to the tissues, and exhalation eliminates the waste product (carbon dioxide), making room for fresh air. This is a continuous process that takes place without us even thinking about it.

We must breathe in the spiritual also. The first step is inspiration, as explained in 2 Timothy 3:16: "All scripture is given by *inspiration* of God…" (emphasis mine). The word *inspiration* in that verse means "God breathed." There must be a continual flow of His Spirit to breathe the Word of God into our hearts, then to cleanse us and empty us of the impurities of daily life.

In the natural body, there are several things that can affect the process of breathing, hindering the flow of air, such as an upper airway obstruction or various types of lung disease. One of the first things taught in a CPR course is that the airway must be open (with nothing blocking the flow of air), and that the most common cause of airway obstruction is the tongue.

Likewise, in the spiritual sense, the tongue is an unruly member that must be controlled. This can only be done by God, for no man can tame the tongue (James 3:8). If we yield the control of our tongue to Him, then the Holy Spirit can flow into us with a forceful blast and revive us, giving us a life that is pleasing to God.

The parable of the sower in Mark 4 lists several other things that can cause choking. Verse 19 informs us that "the cares of this world, and the deceitfulness of riches, and the lusts of other things entering in, choke the word.…" We need to allow God to remove such things from our lives, as they obstruct the flow of the Spirit. At times He may even need to chasten us with a spiritual "Heimlich" maneuver!

Emphysema, or COPD (chronic obstructive pulmonary disease), occurs gradually. Over time, the lungs become stiff and unyielding, affecting the ability to move air in and out; but nothing actually blocks the airway. This illness develops as a result of years of exposure to pollutants such as cigarette smoke or other toxic air contaminants such as smoke, dust, or asbestos.

If we continually allow our spirits to be exposed to the pollutants of this world instead of exposing them to the God-breathed, inspired Scriptures, then we, too, will become stiff and unyielding, hindering the flow of the Holy Spirit.

Due to the obstruction of alveoli (air sacs) in the lungs, which occurs with the development of emphysema, these patients have a difficult time exhaling carbon dioxide, the waste product of metabolism, and this allows it to build up in the bloodstream, affecting their health. The air sacs (alveoli) are that part of the lung in which the exchange of carbon dioxide and oxygen takes place, thereby causing the person with this disease to also become low in oxygen and short of breath with minimal exertion. This, of course, would severely restrict their ability to run, even if they wanted to. In addition, "air trapping" occurs, resulting in a "barrel-chested" appearance.

Likewise, in the spiritual sense, if we are affected by this type of lung disease, we will tend to only take in that part of the Word of God that makes us feel good, failing to lay hold of the necessary Scriptures that enable us to empty out ourselves of things that hinder us from running the race. Without the doctrine, reproof, and correction of the Word (2

Tim. 3:16), we become "puffed up" with pride (2 Cor. 5:2), or "barrel-chested" with spiritual emphysema.

In contrast to emphysema, pneumonia is a lung disease that occurs rapidly after contact with an infecting organism. The infection spreads rapidly, and the victim suddenly experiences difficulty breathing. Fluid builds up in the air sacs (alveoli) and must be removed, as it is blocking the ability to take in oxygen.

Spiritually, we may find ourselves suddenly overwhelmed by circumstances, feeling as though we are drowning, with no way out of our troubles. But God is faithful to intervene if we will let Him, as we read in 1 Corinthians 10:13: "...God is faithful, who will not suffer [allow] you to be tempted [tested] above that ye are able; but will with the temptation also make a way to escape, that ye may be able to bear it."

If we sit at Jesus' feet and breathe in the life-giving oxygen of His Word, we will not only escape, but we will become more than conquerors through the Word. Jesus was able to overcome Satan in the wilderness through the Word when He was in a physically weakened state. That same Word is also *our* source of power and life, no matter how severe the trial.

In the medical treatment of pneumonia, chest percussion, along with antibiotics, can be used to shake the fluid loose from the lungs and allow it to drain. This is done by first pounding on the chest with cupped hands over the affected area and then having the patient lie head-down across the bed to allow drainage by gravity. Spiritually this is accomplished by humbling ourselves and yielding to the hand of the Lord, through His testing and perhaps chastening, to rid us of self, pride, and the things of the world or the old creation that have crept in and infected us.

Heb. 12:1 encourages us to "...run with patience the race that is set before us", which, of course, is difficult to do unless you have healthy lungs. Long distance runners learn to pace themselves so they can run at the right speed to take in adequate oxygen during the race to supply the needs of their body and their muscles as they contract. Otherwise, if they are running too fast, they will soon need to slow down, or perhaps even stop for a while, in order to get enough oxygen to avoid collapsing.

We must be careful, therefore, not to get ahead of the Lord, or we, too, will fall flat on our faces gasping for air. As Paul instructed, we must learn to run with *patience*, keeping pace with the Holy Spirit, who is our breath, allowing Him to flow through us constantly and to renew our strength along the way so that we can run and not be weary (Isa. 40:31).

In addition to running with patience, as runners we must wear loose clothing and strip ourselves of anything that would restrict our ability to take a deep breath. We are also told in Hebrews 12:1 to "...lay aside every weight, and the sin which doth so easily beset us." Paul warned the Galatian racers that the heavy burden of the law would need to be laid down in order to run the race to win: "Ye did run well; who did hinder you?" (Gal. 5:7). They had become entangled again with the yoke of legality and were no longer able to breathe freely due to all the restrictions. As a result, they had stopped running. They needed to be set free from the restrictive cloak of the law, which they had previously laid aside, in order to resume running; and so must we.

The ability to run to win Christ does not come from our own self-effort, but through the power of the Holy Spirit as we breathe in the Word of His grace. That means that all we need to do is continue to breathe in deeply the inspired Word and run in the liberty wherewith Christ has made us free. So, let us run that we may obtain the prize. First Corinthians 9:24 states: "Know ye not that they which run in a race run all, but one receiveth the prize? So run, that ye may obtain."

SPIRITUAL ABSCESSES

What is an abscess? It is a localized collection of pus that is walled off inside the body. It is usually manifested by a lump that is swollen, red, and tender and that may have some drainage. An abscess is commonly caused by bacteria under the skin or foreign bodies that the immune system walls off and attacks with white cells to keep it from spreading. A common example would be a boil. Abscesses need to be drained in order to heal completely or they will keep coming back. If left untreated, they continue to grow and can even burst and spread the infection.

An example in the Bible of a physical abscess is seen in the story of Job, who was afflicted with boils on his entire body when God allowed Satan to test Job's integrity and faithfulness (Job 2:7). He was covered with painful draining sores that would not heal. Job's friends suggested all kinds of spiritual remedies and tried to get Job to confess his secret sin, but in the end, he was healed when he repented of his attitude toward them, prayed for them, and accepted God's sovereign will for his life. Likewise, our spiritual abscesses will be healed through obedience to God's Word, as will be explained in this discussion of abscesses and their treatment.

Sometimes abscesses are hidden and not visible on the surface because they are deep inside the body. This kind of abscess can be life-threatening and must be treated surgically without delay. Examples of this type would be an abscess in the kidney, a ruptured appendix, or a diverticular abscess (a pus pocket on the colon). These are usually diagnosed with a CT scan when the patient presents to the emergency room with abdominal pain, fever, or other symptoms of a serious infection. I personally have experienced, in my sixties, a ruptured appendix with a large abscess, and I can attest to the severe pain and weakness it causes. I required lifesaving surgery to remove the appendix and abscess and to drain it.

An abscess can occur quickly or slowly depending on the cause. Sometimes it occurs as a result of something that happened years ago, such as an accident with embedded glass or other foreign material that the body has walled off. It may cause few symptoms initially, until it finally reaches the surface and starts draining. Drainage from an abscess can be rather foul-smelling and not pleasant to deal with, but it must take place in order to heal.

There are things in our lives that we sometimes are not fully aware of that may be affecting us spiritually. Or perhaps there are things that we suppress or ignore because we don't consider them to be that much of a problem, or really that bad. However, just like an abscess, they will keep on festering until they finally "come to a head" and have to be dealt with.

When my appendix festered, forming an abscess, I didn't think my abdominal pain was bad enough to be concerned about at first. I thought I just had gas from eating too many turnips or that it was due to my new vitamins. Several days later, I realized I was in trouble and went to the emergency room for treatment. Because of my delay, I was quite ill by that time as the appendix had already ruptured, and I had signs of sepsis, requiring immediate surgery.

In like manner spiritual abscesses can make us weak and unable to have victory over Satan, or they can mar our Christian testimony. These abscesses, too, must be opened and drained so that we can be healed. The smell of that drainage may be just as unpleasant as a physical abscess. At times we may wish that we had left it alone, for it can be offensive to others as we are in the process of healing. However painful it may be to us, there is no other way to restore our spiritual health and strength.

There is a picture in the Old Testament of a spiritual abscess that resulted in overwhelming defeat when Israel went to battle against the people of Ai. This is recorded in Joshua 7. Israel had just won a mighty victory against Jericho and became lifted up with pride, thinking they only needed a few thousand men instead of their whole army to win the next battle. Not only was that a problem, but there was a deeper, hidden sin that was brought to light when Joshua prayed to God for the answer. God revealed to him that there was sin in the camp in verse 11: "Israel hath sinned, and they have also transgressed my covenant which I have commanded them: for they have even taken of the accursed thing."

Achan finally confessed, after an investigation, and said in verse 21: "When I saw among the spoils [of Jericho] a goodly Babylonish garment, and two hundred shekels of silver, and a wedge of gold of fifty shekels weight, then I coveted them, and took them; and, behold, they are hid in the earth in the midst of my tent, and the silver under it."

First he saw, then he coveted, then he took and then hid them; but they were not hidden from God, nor could the sin be hidden from Him. This was a spiritual abscess that had to be opened and drained in order to heal the sickness that it had brought upon the whole camp of Israel.

God wants to heal us from the inside out, to cleanse our secret faults so that we may live a life of victory, but we must be willing to go to Him for the healing. There were many steps to Achan's sin: seeing, coveting, taking, and finally hiding it. This is also true for us. However, God is able to intervene at any stage along the progression of the formation of an abscess. If we take our eyes off of Christ, we will soon begin to desire the things of the world. Anything that distracts us from our "first love" can be a hindrance to overcoming, even if it is the *good* things in our lives: our jobs, our families, our friends, or our accomplishments. None of these things would be considered sinful in and of themselves, but they could trigger the formation of an abscess if they take precedence over the Lord.

King David committed a similar sin to Achan's in 2 Samuel 11. He had stayed home rather than going out to battle, and one evening as he was walking on his rooftop he saw a woman bathing herself. Instead of turning away, he continued to look, then to covet.

Sometimes things can momentarily attract our attention, perhaps by accident, but we do not need to keep staring at them. This is one of the pitfalls of pornography on the internet. You may be accidentally exposed to it, but Satan tempts you to keep looking until it has you trapped, and soon a spiritual abscess is formed.

David continued to gaze upon the woman and to lust after her, then he sent for her and committed adultery. But it didn't end there, for she became pregnant. Now he had to do something drastic to hide his sin, because her husband was away from home on the battlefield, where David should have been; therefore, the child could not be his.

The abscess was now beginning to grow and become painful, so David had to devise a new plan. The end result was that David actually committed murder, by proxy, by having her husband placed on the front lines of the battle, where he was killed. After that, David took Bathsheba to be his wife. He thought the problem was solved.

David had been called "a man after God's own heart," but now David's heart needed cleansing. Even those who are running the race to win Christ can be tripped up by Satan and fall. God is still faithful; He is willing and ready to heal our spiritual abscess whenever we are willing to give it to Him.

God sent the prophet Nathan to speak God's Word to David. Nathan spoke a parable from God that made David angry (see 2 Sam. 12). It brought to the surface the abscess that was hidden, thereby causing David great pain. The Word of God searches our hearts and pierces down deep inside to the abscess like the surgeon's scalpel. Hebrews 4:12 states, "For the word of God is quick [living], and powerful, and sharper than any twoedged sword, piercing even to the dividing asunder of soul and spirit...." David's sin was cleansed when he confessed and repented, but he still had to live with that surgical scar.

In order to treat a physical abscess, a doctor must perform an I&D (incision and drainage). The doctor usually takes a #11 blade scalpel to do this, which is shaped like a dagger, having a sharp edge on both sides (a two-edged sword). The blade is used to pierce down into the depths of the abscess, releasing the foul-smelling pus that has built up. The longer it has been there, the worse it smells, due to the action of anaerobic bacteria over time. All the dead flesh must be cut away, and if a foreign body is present, it must also be removed. After that, the wound is flushed out with sterile saline. Finally, either a drain is inserted or the wound is packed to allow it to heal from the inside out.

Likewise, in the spiritual we must first recognize our need and go to the Great Physician. Psalm 139:23–24 states: "Search me, O God, and know my heart: try me, and know my thoughts: and see if there be any wicked way in me."

As I previously mentioned, a doctor must explore the abscess and remove any foreign bodies in order for healing to take place, or it will re-form. First of all, what is a foreign body? It is anything inside your body that doesn't belong there, such as a splinter or a piece of glass. Your body will recognize it as foreign and begin to wall it off with white cells, resulting in pus accumulation and infection.

So, what are spiritual foreign bodies? They are things that don't belong in a Christian's life. They belong to the old creation and need to be removed by the scalpel of God's Word.

Ephesians 4:31 gives us a list of several foreign bodies that must be taken out: "Let all bitterness, and wrath, and anger, and clamor, and evil speaking, be put away from you, with all malice." These things also need to be flushed out with the "washing of the water of the word" (Eph. 5:26), in order that we may be presented to Him as a spotless bride that is holy and without blemish (Eph. 5:27), having no abscesses.

Do you seem to have a "hot button" that people can push and make you angry? Perhaps you have a hidden abscess that is painful and sore when touched and is in need of the two-edged sword to drain it. Some common issues like these are jealousy, unforgiveness, holding a grudge, prejudice, or pride. These things can not only affect you spiritually but can make you physically ill if not dealt with. Hebrews 12:15 tells us to beware lest a root of bitterness springs up within us and troubles us.

Ephesians 4:29 warns us, "Let no corrupt communication proceed out of your mouth." That is not just referring to profanity; it also means no judging or putting someone down, but instead lifting them up.

God wants to empty out our foul-smelling abscess and pack it with Ephesians 4:32: "And be ye kind one to another...even as God for Christ's sake hath forgiven you." These are the characteristics of the new creation that are pleasing to God and that produce a sweet-smelling aroma to those around us.

Spiritual abscesses can also occur in a church body, as seen in the Corinthian church in 1 Corinthians 5:1. This abscess was easily diagnosed by the apostle Paul, for it was not hidden; in fact, it was on the surface for everyone to see. He stated that it was commonly reported among them that there was fornication involving one of their members and his father's wife. In spite of the foul smell coming from this abscess, everyone seemed to be accepting it or ignoring it. They had not sought the Lord to get rid of it. Paul not only diagnosed it, but he told them that God's remedy was to remove the person from fellowship, allowing the abscess to be drained. The man later repented and was healed and restored to fellowship.

Sometimes there are abscesses in churches regarding favoritism, backbiting, hurtful talk, and judging others instead of ourselves. We should be praying for each other, lifting up the hands that hang down and building up the weaker saints instead of treading on them. We need not only to *preach* grace but to *show* grace.

"Having therefore these promises, dearly beloved, let us cleanse ourselves from all filthiness of the flesh and spirit, perfecting holiness in the fear of God" (2 Cor. 7:1). We are also admonished by Paul in 1 Corinthians 11:28 to examine *ourselves*. So, let us do a spiritual body self-exam to check for tender, painful areas that could indicate abscesses in need of drainage. Don't allow a hidden abscess to rob you of a victorious Christian walk. Instead, submit yourself to the discerning and healing power of the sharp, two-edged scalpel of the Word to drain that abscess.

It is equipped with two edges that will bring healing:

> 1 John 1:9: "If we confess our sins, he is faithful and just to forgive us our sins, and to cleanse us from all unrighteousness."

> James 5:16: "Confess your faults one to another, and pray one for another, that ye may be healed."

SPIRITUAL ARTHRITIS

What is arthritis? It is a physical condition that affects the joints, causing pain, stiffness, or swelling. It is the leading cause of disability in the United States because it affects the normal functioning of the body. Arthritis can affect us both physically and spiritually. I am going to discuss the joints in the natural body and how arthritis affects them so we can better understand the spiritual.

How is a joint constructed? It is not just bone against bone, for there is cartilage that acts like a cushion between the bones. Joint fluid, called synovial fluid, lubricates and allows free movement without friction. A joint is held together by ligaments, and muscles and tendons surround the joint to stabilize it and allow it to move and act like a lever to perform work.

We are joined together in a specific manner (fitly joined together) for a purpose both physically and spiritually. Ephesians 4:15–16 says, "But speaking the truth in love, may grow up into him in all things, which is the head, even Christ: From whom the whole body *fitly joined* together and compacted by that which every joint supplieth, according to the effectual working in the measure of every part, maketh increase of the body unto the edifying [building up] of itself in love" (emphasis mine).

What is that which every joint supplies? It is the synovial fluid and the cartilage, the lubricant and the cushion. The joint fluid represents the Holy Spirit that flows in the body of Christ. The cartilage is the cushion between the bones in the joint that keeps them from rubbing against each other and causing pain. Do you sometimes feel like *you* are that cartilage that is always being squeezed? God may be using you as a "peacemaker" to prevent friction between two other members in the body. No wonder the Scripture says, "Blessed are the peace makers"!

Joints are wonderful when they work properly. When they don't, we call that arthritis. First Corinthians 1:10 describes a healthy joint: "Now I beseech you, brethren, by the name of our Lord Jesus Christ, that ye all speak the same thing, and that there be no divisions [friction] among you; but that ye be *perfectly joined* together [no deformity, no ligament tears, not bowlegged, or knock-kneed, no disabling pain] in the same mind [the mind of Christ]..." (emphasis mine). The mind of Christ is to do the will of the Father and not insist on our own way, with no arguing or complaining.

Verse 11 gives us a picture of an abnormal, unhealthy joint. Paul states that it had been declared to him that there were contentions among them (inflammation, impaired mobility, creaking, popping, groaning, arguing, friction in the joints). Believe me, an arthritic joint will complain to you when you try to make it move and do something. In fact, it can be quite noisy. This is true in both the natural and spiritual.

We are joined together in the physical and spiritual body by joints to allow the body to move and do work and stand. Without joints, the body would be rigid and unmovable.

Arthritis affects the function of these joints and therefore the whole body. Satan cannot destroy the body of Christ, so he tries to keep it from being able to function smoothly by causing divisions and contentions among its members.

What are some of the symptoms of arthritis, and how does it hinder us physically and spiritually? Due to painful joints in the hands and shoulders, it may be hard to even perform your basic activities of daily living, such as dressing, bathing, or even feeding yourself. Knee and hip pain could impair your ability to walk, and especially to run, and could also increase the risk of falling. If you fell, it would be difficult to get back up. Even getting up out of a chair might be a challenge. Back pain could affect your ability to carry things or to stand or sit very long.

How about spiritually? Would we be able to don our spiritual armor, as described in Ephesians 6, or to even be able to stand fast against Satan? Or grip our sword, which is the Word of God? How would we "lay hold" of eternal life if we lost the function of our hands? What about "walking in the light" or "running the race that is set before us"? How could we bear one another's burdens (or even our own)? Those things would be impossible based on our own abilities, but praise God, there is help available from the Great Physician!

There are two main categories of arthritis: degenerative and inflammatory.

Degenerative arthritis is called osteoarthritis and is the most common type. It occurs with age and overuse of a joint or previous injury. It is sometimes referred to as "wear and tear" arthritis. Due to years of overwork, the cartilage at the ends of the bones wears out, and the ligaments become frayed and tear, resulting in an unstable joint and pain from bone rubbing against bone. It also causes creaking and popping that can be felt and sometimes heard audibly.

Spiritually this is also caused by overwork. Yes, we are created in Christ Jesus unto good works, but our works must be according to the Holy Spirit's leading and not according to our own zeal. We cannot add anything to the work of salvation, because it was finished on the cross by Christ, who loudly proclaimed, "It is finished." Any works that we do now are for the purpose of glorifying Christ, and that leaves no room for boasting.

Let us consider the story of Mary and Martha in Luke 10:38–42. Martha became irritated with her sister, Mary, who was sitting at Jesus' feet and listening to His words, while Martha was left to try to prepare a meal for Jesus all by herself. She became so upset she went to Jesus and complained to Him, wanting Him to tell Mary to get up and help her. Jesus didn't want a dinner; He wanted fellowship and He still does today. Sometimes churches or individuals become so overzealous in trying to do things *for* God that they have no time to spend *with* Him. There is no time left to listen to that still, small voice or to sit at Jesus' feet to rest and take in the Word of God.

Being overly concerned with good works can cause friction between members of the body of Christ. Martha was suffering from spiritual arthritis. Jesus informed her how to cure her arthritis: She would need to cease from her own works even as God did from His and enter into rest as Mary had already done (Heb. 4:10).

Stephen, in his sermon in Acts 7:51, calls the religious people stiff necked: "Ye stiff necked and uncircumcised in heart and ears, ye do always resist the Holy Ghost." He boldly diagnosed them with spiritual arthritis. Arthritis causes a stiff neck both physically and spiritually. It is hard to bow your head with a stiff neck. It is also hard to look up. We need to bow to the will of God and "look up," for our redemption (deliverance) is drawing nigh. You can also get a stiff neck from looking back too much. We are to forget those things that are behind and not keep looking back.

Inflammatory arthritis occurs when your body's immune system becomes overactive and starts attacking your own tissues in the joints instead of the bacteria, viruses, and other foreign bodies that invade the system. This results in red or painful, inflamed, swollen joints that can eventually lead to joint destruction if not treated.

It can be triggered by certain medications, by viruses, by toxic chemical exposure, or for unknown reasons. The bacteria that causes strep throat can trigger an autoimmune response if the disease is not treated, and it can attack the joints, heart, or kidneys. We call this rheumatic fever. The classic example of inflammatory arthritis is rheumatoid arthritis, and it even occurs in children. Age is not a factor.

We are constantly being exposed by Satan to the toxins of this world, for he is seeking to devour us. We can become so entangled with the affairs of this life and the pleasures of this world that there is no time for church or Bible study. Soon our love for the Lord and the rest of the body of Christ begins to grow cold and triggers spiritual arthritis. Spiritually it manifests itself when one member of the body becomes inflamed against another for any reason or due to unconfessed sin.

Galatians 5:14–15 instructs us: "For all the law is fulfilled in one word, even in this; Thou shalt love thy neighbor as thyself; But, if ye bite and devour one another, take heed that ye be not consumed one of another." This is joint destruction, which impairs the function of the body and causes pain. One member becomes inflamed against another due to lack of love. Paul tells us in Galatians 6:1–2 that if a man be overtaken in a fault, we are to restore him in love and bear one another's burdens. We are to build up, not tear down or destroy. Without God's love, that is not possible.

We are also advised by Paul in Ephesians 4:25–32 that we are members one of another and that we should not give place to the devil when we are angry. The devil tries to cause bitterness, wrath, and uncontrolled anger between members, which leads to joint destruction and impairment of the body of Christ.

David prayed in Psalm 6:2–3: "...heal me for my bones are vexed...my soul is also sore vexed [sore and inflamed]." He had unconfessed sin in his life, but he was healed when he repented.

What are some situations that can make the pain of arthritis worse? Sitting too long causes stiffness. The Bible never says to "sit still and see the salvation of the Lord." It says to "stand" or "walk"; to "walk in the spirit." But over-work without taking time to rest will cause a flareup of joint pain and swelling. Jesus would often leave the crowds of people and opportunities to minister to them and find a quiet place alone to commune with His Father. We must remember to do the same. In addition to prolonged sitting, cold can also cause stiffness. Our hearts will become cold if we forsake the assembling of ourselves together. We need the fellowship of one another and encouragement from the Word.

How do we treat arthritis in the natural body? When I first started my medical practice, aspirin or its derivatives were the primary treatment for arthritis, along with steroids. Neither of these could be used for very long due to their long-term side effects, such as ulcers. Then along came a class of medications called NSAIDs (nonsteroidal anti-inflammatory drugs), such as Motrin (ibuprofen) and Aleve (naproxen), which are now over the counter. These are helpful for the pain and swelling of osteoarthritis, but they do not prevent the wearing out of the cartilage. Currently research is being done on a drug that can help prevent the progression of osteoarthritis, but none is available yet.

For inflammatory arthritis, such as rheumatoid arthritis, we use disease-modifying drugs like methotrexate and plaquenil, or a new class of drugs called "biologics" that keep the immune system from being overactive and help prevent joint destruction.

One of the quickest treatments for an acutely painful joint such as a knee or shoulder is to inject the joint with a steroid, which is a strong anti-inflammatory agent, putting the medicine directly where the problem is.

Hebrews 4:12 declares to us that the Word of God is quick (living) and powerful and sharper than any two-edged sword and is able to pierce into our innermost being, including the joints. The Word of God is the sharp needle that injects the steroid, but what is the steroid? The answer is found in Galatians 5:14: "...thou shat love thy neighbor as thyself." Love is the anti-inflammatory agent that needs to be injected into the inflamed, painful spiritual joint in the body of Christ through the Holy Spirit, which is the syringe. The love of God is shed abroad in our hearts by the Holy Ghost. Only God's love can heal the bitterness and anger with which Satan tries to attack us in order to disable the body of Christ.

What if you are currently suffering physical pain from arthritis in your natural body, and the healing just doesn't seem to come? Paul prayed for the thorn in his flesh to be removed, but God didn't do it. Instead He promised, "my grace is sufficient" (see 2 Cor. 12:7–10). Jesus knows exactly how you feel. He experienced excruciating joint pain on the cross for you. It says in the messianic Psalm 22:14: "... all my bones are out of joint...." The act of crucifixion caused His shoulders to be pulled out of joint. He could not hold Himself up with His feet due to the nail in them, which caused severe foot pain with pressure. The nails in His hands were actually placed in the wrists (the carpal tunnel area), where the median nerve is located, causing severe pain and spasms in the hands. The nail in His feet caused a similar problem with the nerve in the tarsal tunnel at the ankle.

We have a High Priest who is touched by the feeling of our infirmities, because as a man He also suffered physical pain. He understands and cares. His grace is sufficient for you in your trial. His grace and love are also sufficient for spiritual arthritis if we allow God's Word to pierce into the inflamed joints and inject His love through the power of the Holy Spirit.

The body of Christ need not be disabled from spiritual arthritis. Instead of creaking and popping and complaining, we need to be walking in the Spirit and running the race. Why not call the Great Physician for your heavenly joint injection today?

DEADLY SNAKE BITES: SPIRITUAL ANTIVENOM

And the LORD sent fiery serpents among the people, and they bit the people; and much people of Israel died. Therefore, the people came to Moses, and said, We have sinned, for we have spoken against thee; pray unto the LORD, that he take away the serpents from us. And Moses prayed for the people. And the LORD said unto Moses, Make thee a fiery serpent, set it upon a pole: and it shall come to pass, that every one that is bitten, when he looketh upon it, shall live. And Moses made a serpent of brass, and put it upon a pole, and it came to pass, that if a serpent had bitten any man, when he beheld the serpent of brass, he lived.

—Numbers 21:6–9

We see in this account of the children of Israel in the wilderness that they had sinned against the Lord, and God sent fiery serpents among them as judgment. We know that these were deadly poisonous snakes because many of the people died. When this happened, they repented of their sin and cried out for God to remove the serpents.

Because God is a righteous Judge, He could not take away His judgment for sin, but He could, and did, make a way of escape for all who chose to listen and obey. He commanded Moses to make a serpent of brass and to place it upon a pole to be lifted up for all to see. If any person was bitten, all they had to do was to look upon the brazen serpent and they would live.

The serpent on the pole, which today is used as a doctor's symbol for healing, is taken from this scripture passage in Numbers. However, it has a much deeper meaning than that to us spiritually.

This method of healing seems to be a very unusual thing for God to use. Why would He send poisonous serpents as judgment to give the "sting of death" and then use another serpent, made of brass, to take away that sting? As I will explain, God, the Great Physician, created and administered the first spiritual antivenom through this strange act.

In the emergency room, a victim of a poisonous snake bite is given antivenom to counteract the venom that has been injected into his bloodstream through the snake's fangs, to thus prevent death. But where does antivenom come from?

In the manufacture of antivenom, the venom of a poisonous snake is intentionally injected into an animal, which then produces antibodies against it. Blood from the animal is then removed, and the lifesaving serum is separated out of it. This serum has the ability to neutralize the poison. In other words, the blood of an animal who has received the "sting of death" can give life to a person who has been bitten, who would otherwise die without hope.

"And as Moses lifted up the serpent in the wilderness, even so must the son of man be lifted up: That whosoever believeth in him should not perish, but have eternal life" (John 3:14–15). These verses explain to us that the serpent of brass on the pole was a picture of Christ, the Redeemer, who was lifted up on the cross that we may look to Him and live. This is further confirmed in John 12:32–33, when Jesus said, "And I, if I be lifted up from the earth, will draw all men unto me. This he said, signifying what death he should die," referring to His death on the cross.

His death on the cross provided healing for our sin-sick souls and neutralized the poison of Satan. Jesus Christ, who knew no sin, had to be made sin for us in order that we could be made righteous, as we read in 2 Corinthians 5:21–22. Jesus, as seen in the book of Numbers, was pictured as a serpent of brass on a pole. Brass, in Scripture, speaks of judgment, so the brazen serpent signifies that God's judgment for our sin was poured out upon Christ on the cross, as He was made sin.

The apostle Paul tells us in 1 Corinthians 15:56 that "the sting of death is sin; and the strength of sin is the law." Under the Mosaic Law, the penalty for sin was death; Ezekiel 18:4 states: "…the soul that sinneth, it shall die." We are *all* condemned to death because Romans 3:23 declares that "all have sinned, and come short of the glory of God."

However, God has provided the lifesaving antidote for the sting of death. After Adam and Eve sinned in the Garden of Eden by disobeying God and partaking of the forbidden fruit, God gave the first promise of redemption. It was given in the form of a prophecy that was directed to the serpent (Satan) in Genesis 3:15: "And I will put enmity between thee [Satan] and the woman, and between thy seed and her seed; it [the woman's seed] shall bruise thy head, and thou shalt bruise his heel."

A snakebite victim is not always able to identify the type of snake that bit him, and therefore he may not know whether or not it was poisonous. There are several important signs that a doctor looks for during the examination of the bite area that give clues as to whether or not the fangs of the snake have injected poisonous venom, even if the patient is not yet ill. Poisonous snake venom contains a substance that affects the walls of the blood vessels causing them to become leaky, resulting in hemorrhage into the tissues around the bite. This produces rapid swelling and ecchymosis (a bruised appearance). By these signs, the doctor can diagnose the bite as poisonous and order the antivenom (also called antivenin or antivenim) and begin treatment as soon as possible before shock and death occur.

The description given in Genesis 3:15 is a graphic and scientifically accurate picture of the wound of someone who has stepped on the head of a poisonous snake and in so doing was bitten in the heel. We know, because of the bruising that was mentioned, that the heel wound was a deadly one.

Sin entered into the world through Adam, and all mankind was placed under the sentence of death. First Corinthians 15:22 tells us, "For as in Adam all die, even so in Christ shall all be made alive." Without this promise, we would have no hope. Adam had been bitten by the fiery serpent (Satan) and needed antivenom to escape eternal death. But Christ, the seed of the woman, willingly allowed Himself to be bitten (to be made sin for us), and then He gave His blood as spiritual antivenom that we might live.

The good news is that it doesn't stop there. At the same time, by His death on the cross, He crushed the head (the authority) of the serpent, Satan, so that he no longer has the power to destroy us.

All that is required for us to receive that antivenom is to first acknowledge that we, too, have sinned (have been bitten) and then look to the One who was made sin for us on the cross. When we partake of the lifegiving blood of Christ by accepting Him as Savior, then we receive the gift of eternal life.

SPIRITUAL IMPOTENCE

Acts 14:8–10 records the healing of an impotent man: "And there sat a certain man at Lystra, impotent in his feet, being a cripple from his mother's womb, who never had walked: The same heard Paul speak: who steadfastly beholding him, and perceiving that he had faith to be healed, Said with a loud voice, Stand upright on thy feet. And he leaped and walked."

The word *impotent* means "loss of power" or the "inability to stand upright." I am going to compare a physical condition called "impotence" or "erectile dysfunction" with this biblical example of the man's loss of power and his inability to stand upright, and then contrast it with a similar spiritual condition seen in the church today. The physical condition of impotence (erectile dysfunction) results in a loss of power and inability to stand upright. In addition to this, it can cause the loss of ability to reproduce or to be fruitful.

Spiritual impotence would indicate a loss of power and ability to stand against Satan. This condition is described by Paul in 2 Timothy 3:5: "Having a *form* of godliness, but denying the *power* thereof." Organized religion today seems to be more concerned with form than function. It may appear to be godly, but it is not manifesting God's power. Likewise, in the natural, an impotent man *looks* the same as any other man upon physical examination. He has a form but no power to perform.

What are some of the causes of physical impotence, and how do they apply to us spiritually? Basically, impotence can be caused by any disease that affects the circulation or blood supply to the pelvic and genital region, or that affects the desire to be intimate. That would include such diseases as diabetes, hypertension, hardening of the arteries, anxiety, or even trauma. In addition, there are certain medications used to treat these conditions that can cause impotence as a side effect. Alcohol use can also result in impotence. We are told in Leviticus 17:11 that "the life of the flesh is in the blood.... It is the blood that maketh atonement for the soul." This is both a medically and a spiritually accurate statement, for without the blood there is no life for body or soul.

This is especially true regarding impotence. The reproductive organs in the pelvic area require an overabundance of blood supply to function, not just enough to keep from dying. With a complete lack of blood supply, an organ or body part would die, and with an inadequate supply, there is loss of the ability to function properly, even though it appears normal.

Some people are satisfied with just enough truth to be saved, and they have no desire for an intimate, dynamic relationship with the Lord. They believe that the blood of Jesus brings salvation but nothing more. They limit the flow of the blood in their lives, and therefore the power is lacking. They only desire enough blood to keep from dying.

The blood of Jesus never loses its power, but sometimes we fail to lay hold of the abundance of power within it. Some churches today preach a bloodless gospel; they want to avoid a "slaughterhouse" religion. They have even removed from their hymnbooks all of the old songs about the blood, such as "Power in the Blood" and "Nothing but the Blood," in order to keep from offending anyone. As we read in Hebrews 10:29, they have "counted the blood of the covenant…an unholy thing" and have "…done despite unto the Spirit of grace."

But if we limit the flow of the blood of the crucified Lamb, we have no power in our Christian life. We will be too weak to stand against our enemy, Satan. Paul tells us that the blood not only saves, but that it is our source of power. He wrote these words in 1 Corinthians 1:18: "For the preaching of the cross is to them that perish foolishness; but unto us which are saved it is the power of God."

Samson was given mighty power and strength by God to overcome his enemies, but he became impotent when he began to trust in the flesh. He began to feel confident in himself instead of relying on God for his strength. He became "intoxicated" by a worldly lifestyle and yielded to an ungodly woman; as a result, he was weakened both physically and spiritually. He had to come to a place of utter debasement and failure before he called upon God to renew his strength. When we wait upon the Lord and allow the power of the blood to flow through us, then He is faithful to renew our strength, as it is promised in Isaiah 40:31. Isaiah 40:29 also declares, "He giveth power to the faint [impotent]; and to them that have no might he increaseth strength."

Another cause of impotence can be due to trauma to the pelvic and groin area that results in injury to the reproductive organs. In Ephesians 6:13–17, we are instructed to protect ourselves with our spiritual armor so that we may be able to stand against Satan. But in particular, relating to impotence, we have been provided with a special girdle to protect our loins (the pelvic area) in verse 14: "Stand therefore having your loins girt about with truth."

God desires that we bear fruit unto Him. The truth of God's Word, especially Paul's gospel, is necessary for our protection and our fruitfulness. It was a result of hearing Paul speak and heeding Paul's word to "stand" that the impotent man in Acts 14 was healed and able to stand upright.

As previously mentioned, anxiety or depression can also be a contributing factor to impotence. Unfortunately, some of the medications that are used to treat these problems can also cause impotence as a side effect and may therefore compound the problem. We are told in Philippians 4:6 to "Be careful [full of care, anxious] for nothing," but instead to pray and give thanks and "...let your requests be made known unto God." If we "cast our cares" upon Him, He will give us peace and joy in place of depression and anxiety.

Nehemiah instructed the people of Israel who were mourning and weeping (Neh. 8:10) to "neither be ye sorry; for the joy of the LORD is your strength." Their strength (their power) was renewed when they began to rejoice in the Lord instead of focusing on their failures and inability to perform God's will.

Viagra was the first in a class of medications called phosphodiesterase inhibitors that were formulated to treat physical impotence, but now there are others. These medications work by causing the blood vessels to relax and dilate, or open up, and allow the blood to flow freely in the pelvic area that was previously lacking an adequate supply.

The modernized church today appears to be suffering from spiritual impotence as they are no longer relying on the power of the blood. They focus more on programs and/or man's ideas in order to draw large crowds, instead of preaching the gospel. As a result, some of the denominational churches are no longer taking a stand against things that God calls sin.

We need not be impotent if we are trusting in the Omnipotent. God has promised to be our source of "spiritual Viagra." The apostle Paul admitted his weakness, but he knew how to tap in to an abundant power supply, for he said in Philippians 4:13: "I can do all things through Christ which strengtheneth me."

We are not powerless against Satan and sin, for we have been given power through the blood to stand upright without fear of falling. Jude reminds us of that in verse 24 of his epistle: "Unto him that is able to keep you from falling, and to present you faultless before the presence of his glory with exceeding joy."

Not only are we given the power to stand, but to be fruitful, as Paul desired and prayed for the saints in Colossians 1:10–11: "That ye might walk worthy of the Lord [walk upright] unto all pleasing, being fruitful in every good work...strengthened with all might, according to his glorious power...."

Abraham was given the power by God physically to be fruitful and become the father of a child at the age of 100 through faith. God had promised that He would have a son, and we read in Romans 4:20 that "he staggered not at the promise of God through unbelief" because he was "fully persuaded that what he [God] had promised, he [God] was able to perform" (v. 21). We know that Abraham was physically impotent, because in verse 19, it states that "he considered not his own body now *dead*…neither yet the deadness of Sara's womb." Abraham was not concerned about *his* own ability to perform, but he relied on *God's* ability to perform.

Likewise, spiritually, in order to overcome impotence, we must be fully persuaded that the blood of Jesus is all that we need. His blood gives life and can restore life to that which was seemingly dead or asleep. We need the wonder-working power of the blood back in the church and in our lives.

God desires for us as His body, the church, that our weakness be made strong, and He desires to have a close, intimate relationship with us through His Son. The blood of Jesus, His very life, was poured out and given to us. His life-blood not only saves us, but it empowers us, for it is the life of Christ in us that enables us to be His chosen, spotless, fruitful bride to reign with Him for eternity.

MURMURING HEARTS

Hebrews 12:11 admonishes us to run with patience the race that is set before us. Prior to engaging in competitive sports, a physical examination needs to be completed to look at the heart, and in particular, to check for murmurs that could indicate a heart problem. Today you are going to have a spiritual sports physical to see if you are able to run the race without fainting. I am going to examine you with the stethoscope of God's Word.

First, I will discuss physical heart murmurs to help you better understand spiritual murmurs. So, what exactly is a murmur? According to *Webster's Dictionary*, it is a low, indistinct sound, a mumbled or muttered complaint, or an abnormal sound in the heart. A murmur in the heart is caused by something that is affecting the free flow of blood, indicating turbulence or resistance to flow.

There are four valves in the heart. They open to allow blood to flow through them and then they close to keep the blood from flowing backward between beats when the heart is at rest. If the blood is flowing freely and the valves are working properly, no sound is made by the valves. But when a valve does not open or close properly, it causes turbulence, creating the sound of a murmur that can be heard with a stethoscope.

A murmur can indicate an underlying heart problem, so a doctor must listen closely for murmurs during an exam. A murmur heard on the *outside* of the body can indicate a problem with the heart on the inside. This is true spiritually as well as physically, "for out of the abundance of the heart the mouth speaketh" (Matt. 12:34). What is inside your heart will be manifested on the outside, especially when you are under stress.

A systolic murmur is the most common type of heart murmur, and it occurs when the heart is beating (working). A diastolic murmur occurs when the heart is at rest, and it is always abnormal, as it indicates that blood is flowing the wrong direction, falling back into the heart chamber, because the valve is not closing properly.

Valve problems can occur due to calcification that has built up, resulting in stiffness, keeping them from moving freely. They become stiff and unyielding. This happens spiritually when we do not yield to the Holy Spirit, but rather resist Him. Infections such as rheumatic fever can cause bacterial immune complexes to accumulate on the edges of the valves and cause scarring and impair their ability to open and close properly. Spiritually this indicates that something from the world has entered into the heart and that the cares of this life are affecting our yielding to the Lord. Jesus said, "*Let* not your heart be troubled" (John 14:1). We have a choice whether or not to let our troubles affect our ability to run the race, or to "cast our cares" on the Lord and *let* Him take care of them.

Murmurs may increase in intensity and become louder with fever, anemia, activity, or anything that causes the heart to work harder. As a doctor, if I am unsure about a murmur, I may have the person jump up and down a few times or run in place to speed up the heart. The harder the heart works, the louder the murmur, so this allows me to hear it better.

You cannot run the race to win with a murmuring heart. From a medical standpoint, if I found a significant murmur, I would have to disqualify you from participating in sports until it was further evaluated by a cardiologist. Likewise, spiritually you can be disqualified from running to win the prize if you are yielding to the flesh and not yielding to the Lord. The apostle Paul stated in 1 Corinthians 9:27: "I keep under my body, and bring it into subjection: lest…I myself should be a castaway [disqualified]." When we yield to the flesh, we develop a murmuring heart.

Let us now examine some examples of murmuring hearts in the Scriptures. First Corinthians 10:10 states: "Neither murmur ye as some of them [in the wilderness]." In Exodus 16:2–3, we read that they murmured against Moses and Aaron because they wanted meat. They were tired of eating manna every day. They were discontented and began resisting God. In verse 8, Moses stated, "…Your murmurings are not against us but against the LORD [God's authority and headship]." They rejected the manna, the bread from heaven, wanting to fulfill the desires of the flesh instead of feasting on Him.

Again, in Psalm 106:24–25: "…they believed not his word: but murmured in their tents, and hearkened not unto the voice of the LORD." Resistance to God's voice, His Word, caused them to murmur spiritually. Hebrews 3:19 informs us that they could not enter the promised land because of unbelief. They wanted to go their own way, much like an abnormal heart valve that allows blood to flow backward, going the wrong direction. Murmuring is unbelief, not appropriating and believing the Word of God.

In John 6:41, the Jews murmured against Jesus because He said, "I am the bread which came down from heaven." They doubted His deity and authority as the Son of God. We are doing the same when we do not allow Him to be the Lord of our lives.

We see a different type of murmur in Acts 6:1: "There arose a murmuring of the Grecians against the Hebrews, because their widows were neglected in the daily ministration." This is the murmuring of jealousy, the feeling that you are being treated unfairly, causing you to demand your own rights.

Paul instructs us in Philippians 2:14 to "Do *all* things without murmurings and disputing." This especially includes the things we do not like to do, the mundane things of our daily home life or occupation, showing love to the unlovely or ungracious, or praying for those who "despitefully use us." We must allow the love of God through the Holy Spirit to flow through us and do His will without murmuring.

I mentioned earlier that increasing activity can increase the intensity of a murmur. Anything that makes the heart work harder or faster will cause an existing murmur to be louder. The Scripture gives us a spiritual example of this in the story of two sisters, Mary and Martha, in Luke 10:38–42. When Jesus visited their home, Martha immediately started preparing a meal for Him, but Mary sat at Jesus' feet and listened to His Word. Martha became upset and complained to Jesus that her sister had left her to serve alone. She wanted Him to tell Mary to get up and help do some of the work. To this Jesus responded, "Martha, Martha, thou art careful and troubled about many things: but one thing is needful: and Mary hath chosen that good part, which shall not be taken from her" (vv. 41–42).

Martha murmured against her sister because she had her eyes on her own works and she was ignoring Jesus. The harder she worked, the louder she murmured and complained. What Jesus really wanted instead of physical food was fellowship. He wants us to sit at His feet and learn of Him, to feast on the Bread from heaven and break bread with Him.

Isaiah 29:24 gives us the cure for our murmuring hearts: "...they that murmured shall learn doctrine." We learn doctrine by studying the Word. This is exactly what Mary was doing, listening to His Word. His Word instructs us that the only way to stop a murmuring heart is to rest in the work that He has already accomplished for us on the cross. If we insist on continuing to do self-works and resisting God's grace, then our murmuring hearts will be heard by the Great Physician and we will be disqualified from running the race to win the prize. So, let us heed His Word and let the Holy Spirit and the love of God flow through us freely, ceasing from our own works even as God did from His. Hebrews 4:10 states: "For he that is entered into his [God's] rest, he also hath ceased from his own works, as God did from his."

SPIRITUAL BIFOCALS
AND CATARACTS

When I got my first pair of bifocals, I realized how important it is to be able to see both near and far. I am going to show you that this is true both physically and spiritually. When we are young, the lens of our eyes is flexible and able to change shape, allowing us to focus an image onto the retina and adjust for different distances. However, the lens is like every other part of our body. As we age, it becomes less flexible. Sooner or later we notice that things are beginning to get a little fuzzy and not quite as clear as they once were. In addition, the lens may gradually become cloudy, making it harder to see, not just to focus. This could indicate the development of cataracts.

At this point, many people simply go to a department store or drugstore and purchase a pair of reading glasses. However, it is also a good idea to see an eye doctor for a complete exam, as decreased vision may also indicate the development of other medical problems such as glaucoma or diabetes that need to be treated. My point is that we need to be able to focus, both physically and spiritually, on things near us or on us as well as things that are farther away. Not only do we need to be able to accommodate for distances, but both of our eyes must be able to focus together so that we do not see double.

If we are nearsighted and can only see close up, it is called "myopia." Peter refers to the spiritual condition of myopia in 2 Peter 1:9: "But he that lacketh these things is blind, and cannot see afar off." In other words, if we have this condition, all we can focus on is ourselves, how we feel and what we need. We become self-centered and perhaps self-conscious, and we begin to worry about how we appear to others or how we appear to God. We become preoccupied with our own self-works, completely forgetting about others around us. We lose sight of the goal and where we are supposed to be focused.

When Peter said in verse 9, "He that lacketh *these things*," to what things is he referring? The answer is found in verses 5 through 7: "And beside this, giving all diligence, add to your faith virtue; and to virtue knowledge; and to knowledge temperance [self-control]; and to temperance patience; and to patience godliness; and to godliness brotherly kindness; and to brotherly kindness charity [love]." These things remind us of the fruit of the Spirit described in Galatians 5:22–23. When we allow the Holy Spirit to work in our lives, "these things" are produced like fruit, and then we are no longer focused on ourselves.

But we do still need to be able to look at ourselves close up in order to "examine ourselves," as is described in 1 Corinthians 11:28. Then we learn that we are in need of a Savior and in need of cleansing by the Word of God and can go to the Lord for that cleansing.

A person who is nearsighted can *only* see close up, and a person who is farsighted can *only* see far away. Neither of these conditions is desirable in the natural or the spiritual. You must be able to see both near and far, hence the need for bifocals. Bifocals have a portion of the lens that allows you to see at a distance and a portion that allows you to see clearly at close range. This is also true spiritually. You need to be able to do both, and so you are in need of spiritual bifocals. There must be a balance in your spiritual life.

We must not remain focused on ourselves and our own circumstances, but we must look beyond them to Jesus. Hebrews 12:2 instructs us to be "looking unto Jesus the author and finisher of our faith" while we are running in the race that is set before us. In other words, He is at the starting line, but He is also our goal, at the finish line, and we must be able to keep our eyes focused on Him in the distance. As racers, we cannot be looking at our own feet or at those around us, but we must keep looking ahead, pressing toward the mark for the prize.

"Faith is the substance of things hoped for, the evidence of things not seen [things that are afar off]" (Heb. 11:1). Hebrews 11:13 tells us that some of the Old Testament believers "died in faith, not having received the promises, but having seen them afar off…embraced them…." Faith was their spiritual bifocals that enabled them to see beyond their present circumstances and lay hold of what God had promised. Without spiritual bifocals, we would not see what God has planned for us, as we would be focused only on ourselves. Through faith, we see through God's eyes and can see the invisible. If God said it in His Word, if He promised it, we know it will happen. We see those things afar off and are no longer nearsighted. When we are no longer focusing on what is happening in the world, then we will not fear the unrest that is around us. Our spiritual bifocals of faith enable us to see beyond ourselves, beyond the present time, and to look for the coming of the Lord. Whether it be near or far, we can see it clearly and embrace it as if it were today.

Now I would like to discuss cataracts and what they mean spiritually. A cataract is the clouding of the lens of the eye, causing it to be no longer crystal clear and resulting in impaired vision. This usually is a result of age, much like the clouding of the headlights on your car. But cataracts can also be caused by trauma, by taking certain medications such as steroids, or from too much unprotected sunlight. According to the World Health Organization (WHO), cataracts are the leading cause of blindness worldwide, just as it likely was in Jesus' day.

Satan has been blinding the eyes of people in the world with spiritual cataracts to keep them from seeing the light of the gospel. This was noted by the apostle Paul in 2 Corinthians 4:3–4: "But if our gospel be hid, it is hid to them that are lost: In whom the god of this world [Satan] hath blinded the minds of them which believe not, lest the light of the glorious gospel of Christ, who is the image of God, should shine unto them."

This is illustrated to us in the physical healing of a blind man by Jesus in Mark 8, whose blindness might, in fact, have been caused by severe cataracts. This miracle is recorded in Mark 8:22–25: "And he [Jesus] cometh to Bethsaida; and they bring a blind man unto him, and besought him to touch him. And he took the blind man by the hand, and led him out of the town; and when he had spit on his eyes, and put his hands upon him, he asked him if he saw ought [anything]. And he looked up, and said, I see men, as trees, walking. After that he put his hands again upon his eyes, and made him look up: and he was restored, and saw every man clearly."

What does the healing of this blind man mean to us spiritually, and why did Jesus do this in such an unusual manner? First of all, we read that He led the man "out of the town" or out of the place of organized religion and the crowds of people. Spiritually we must also separate ourselves from the religious world and be willing to follow Jesus to a place alone with Him, away from the world and the ideas of man.

After they were alone, Jesus did a strange thing: He spit on the man's eyes! What does this mean? Whenever something unusual is recorded in Scripture, it always has an important spiritual meaning. The spit that came out of Jesus' mouth was the water of the Word, for Jesus is the Word. If our eyes are spiritually blind, they can be opened and enlightened by the Word. As we study the Word, we begin to see who Jesus is, that He is not just another man. but the holy Son of God, and we are then brought from darkness into light.

But the blind man at first could not tell Jesus apart from any other man. He could not see Jesus clearly, and neither do we. He could only see "men as trees walking." He looked around and saw men and trees, but the only way he could tell the difference was that some of them were moving. They looked like poles with branches, and he could not tell them apart.

This is a condition like unto severe cataracts in which a person may only see outlines of figures but is not able to recognize people. At this point they are considered legally blind. At first, we see Jesus only as our Savior, but He is much more than that. As we study the Word, He continues to reveal Himself to us further so that we can have a closer relationship with Him.

Jesus touched the blind man's eyes again and instructed him to "Look up," and after doing so he was able to see clearly. We are also instructed in the Word to "look up" and take our eyes off the things of the world: "If ye then be risen with Christ, seek those things which are above…set your affections on things above, not on things on the earth" (Col. 3:1–2).

The Shulamite woman in the Song of Solomon, who is a type of the bride of Christ, was asked, "What is thy beloved more than another beloved…?" (Song 5:9). Because she was now seeking him with her whole heart as a bride does her bridegroom, she described him in detail and then summed up her answer in verse 16: "His mouth [his Word] is most sweet: yea, he is altogether lovely…." When our spiritual eyes have been opened and we "look up," focusing only on His face, then we, too, will see Jesus clearly as our soon coming Lord and beloved Bridegroom.

SPIRITUAL BLOOD TRANSFUSION

Leviticus 17:11 states: "For the life of the flesh is in the blood: and I have given it to you upon the altar to make an atonement for your souls: for it is the blood that maketh an atonement for the soul." In this verse, we see that blood is necessary for both the body and the soul. One of the main physical functions of the blood is to transport oxygen to all the tissues in the body. If a person loses too much blood and it is not replaced, they will die, as oxygen is essential for life. In the Old Testament, under the old covenant, a blood sacrifice was required to make atonement for sin, and without it the penalty was death, for "...without shedding of blood is no remission [of sin]" (Heb. 9:22).

Under the Law, Moses was to sprinkle the blood of the sacrifice on the people, the tabernacle, and all the vessels of ministry. In addition to this, the high priest went into the Holy of Holies once a year on the Day of Atonement to sprinkle blood upon the mercy seat to offer atonement for his own sins and for the sins of the people.

The first blood sacrifice was made when God killed an animal in order to make coats of skin for Adam and Eve after they had sinned in the Garden of Eden. This was a type, or picture, of Christ, who died to clothe us with His righteousness. All the animal sacrifices since that time pointed to the death of Jesus, the Lamb of God, on the cross.

Jesus Himself made reference to that at the Passover supper that He ate with His disciples before He was crucified, in Matthew 26:27–28: "And he [Jesus] took the cup, and gave thanks, and gave it to them, saying, Drink ye all of it; For this is my blood of the new testament, which is shed for many for the remission of sins."

Under the old covenant, the blood was sprinkled on the *outside*, but Jesus was telling them that the blood of the new testament (covenant) was to be applied on the *inside*, for they were to drink it. The wine symbolized His blood, His very life, which He was going to shed for them and for us. It was to be applied internally, spiritually, so that His life would actually enter into them. Today we continue to symbolize that by partaking of communion; however, we actually partake of the life of Christ when we repent of our sins and accept Him as Savior, applying His blood to our hearts.

Receiving a blood transfusion in the natural can save a person from physical death in much the same way as when a person is given life spiritually by accepting the blood of Jesus as atonement for their sins. The average adult has between 4.5 to 5.5 liters of blood, or 1.2 to 1.5 gallons, depending on the person's weight. If you lose large amounts of blood—one-half to two-thirds of your total blood volume—you will go into shock and die. Therefore, blood transfusions can save lives, so blood donors are desperately needed. In fact, according to the Red Cross, each year 4.5 million lives are saved by blood transfusions. Not everyone has the same blood type, so extreme caution must be taken to be sure a person receives the correct type or a fatal transfusion reaction could occur. Blood type O-negative is considered the universal donor type and is in great demand, as it does not contain any AB antigens and it can be transfused into anyone in an emergency situation.

First of all, a donor must willingly "shed" his own blood in order to give life to another. Then the person in need of it must partake of the blood *personally*. It is not enough for him to know the donor or to love the donor and thank him for the good deed he has done by giving his blood. The blood of the donor must be infused into the recipient's body in order to save his life. Blood cannot be transfused into someone against their will, even if failure to receive it could result in death. It is a personal choice.

Now let us apply this information spiritually. The wrong blood type cannot bring life physically or spiritually. In Hebrews 10:4, we read, "It is not possible that the blood of bulls and goats should take away sins." It could not, therefore, provide eternal life, for it was the wrong blood type. It only covered sin, but it could not take it away. But there is a Donor who has given His blood for us that is compatible. "The Word [Jesus] was made flesh and dwelt among us" (John 1:14). As a man, Jesus could give His blood, and it was able to take away the sins of the world and to give life. His blood is like unto type O-negative, for it is universally compatible for all who are willing to receive it. Jesus offered His life-giving blood to "whosoever will" in John 6:54 and 56 when He was speaking to the people regarding His death on the cross (the donation site): "Whoso...drinketh my blood... dwelleth in me, and I in him." He was telling them, and us, that His blood, His very life, must be taken internally, infused into us by the Holy Spirit, in order to give us eternal life. The life is in the blood, so He is offering us His life, stating that He will personally dwell in us if we will accept His blood.

The recipient of a physical blood transfusion is actually taking the "life" of the donor into their own body after losing their own blood, for the donor blood is now flowing in their veins. When we accept Christ as Savior, we replace the old life (the blood) of the flesh, which was condemned to death, with the new life (the blood) of Christ. We are instructed to "reckon" (count it to be so) ourselves to be dead unto sin but alive unto God through Jesus Christ, as stated in Romans 6:11. If our "old man" is crucified with Him (Rom. 6:6), that means the old creation lost all of its blood just as Jesus did. We can now live because of receiving the life-blood of Jesus and are "alive unto God." Jesus willingly shed His blood as our spiritual donor to give us eternal life, and He offers it to the whole world, to whosoever will. Have you had that life-saving transfusion? First John 5:11–12 states: "And this is the record, that God hath given to us eternal life, and this life is in his Son. He that hath the Son hath life; and he that hath not the Son of God hath not life."

BLINDNESS OF THE HEART

Did you know that every one of us in this world has been blind at one time in our life? We are all blind physically before we are born, because there is no light in the womb. Sight requires light. It must enter through the pupils of our eyes and strike the retina in order to form an image that can be transmitted to the brain. We must be born and enter into the light in order to see. We are likewise spiritually blind until we are born again and the light enters our heart.

The eye is optically equivalent to a camera. A camera also requires light to produce an image. Like a camera, the eye has a lens cover (the eyelid), a variable aperture (opening) to regulate the amount of light that enters (the iris), and a lens that is adjustable for distances and film (the retina). The "film" is "developed" in the brain, initially upside down, but this is automatically corrected in the brain.

Jesus told Nicodemus, a Pharisee, that he needed to be born spiritually (born again) in order to see, just as we must be born physically to have sight, for he had been spiritually blinded by the traditions of his religion. In John 3:3 Jesus states: "Except a man be born again, he cannot *see* the kingdom of God" (emphasis mine). We cannot "see," or understand, spiritual things with our natural minds because we are in darkness and are blinded by Satan, who desires to keep us in the dark.

Second Corinthians 4:4 declares, "The god of this world [Satan] hath blinded the minds of them which believe not, lest the light of the glorious gospel of Christ, who is the image of God, should shine unto them." Romans 1:21 describes the blinded heart of those who reject God: "...their foolish heart was darkened." In addition, the apostle Paul informs the Ephesian saints of the condition of the unbelieving heart before receiving the gospel: "Having the understanding darkened...because of the blindness of their heart" (Eph. 4:18). So, we find that light is essential not only for physical eyes, but also for our spiritual sight.

In Revelation 3:17, God diagnoses the lukewarm church of Laodicea, which represents the religious world of the end times, with spiritual blindness: "Thou sayest, I am rich, and increased with goods, and have need of nothing; and knowest not that thou art wretched, and miserable, and poor, and *blind*, and naked" (emphasis mine). He then offers them a cure for this condition in verse 18: "...anoint thine eyes with eyesalve, that thou mayest see." I am going to discuss the healing of a blind man by Jesus that will illustrate the application of this sight-giving eye salve and how it is provided.

In John 9, Jesus passed by a man who had been blind since birth. Prior to healing this man, He declares, "I am the light of the world," acknowledging the fact that in order to receive sight, the blind man would need to receive light. The healing of this man's eyes was done in an unusual manner in order to illustrate a spiritual truth:

"When he [Jesus] had thus spoken, he spat on the ground, and made clay of the spittle, and he anointed the eyes of the blind man with the clay, And said unto him, Go, wash in the pool of Siloam, (which is by interpretation, Sent). He went his way therefore, and washed, and came seeing" (John 9:6–7). What does all of this mean? First of all, Jesus had to stoop down and mix His spit with the dirt to make clay. The Word of God (Jesus) had to stoop down to leave heaven and come to earth. He took on a body of clay, of flesh, and became a man. The spit that came out of Jesus' mouth represented the water of the Word, as referred to in Ephesians 5:26, which cleanses us. Jesus then put the mud on the man's eyes and told him to go wash. We, too, must recognize the need for cleansing by Jesus' Word and be obedient to His command. Where was the blind man, who represents us, told to go wash? In the pool of Siloam, which means "sent." We must also wash and be made clean in the pool flowing from Calvary, the pool of the One who was *sent* from God to die for our sins. After obeying Jesus' Word and washing in the pool of Siloam, the man received his sight, and so will we.

The washing of the water of the Word gives us sight, for Psalm 119:130 tells us, "The entrance of thy words giveth light," and sight requires light. When we hear the Word of God and apply it personally to our own hearts, our blinded eyes are opened. In Genesis 1:3 we read that God, by His Word, commanded the light to shine unto a world filled with darkness. His Word also does this for us spiritually, as we are told by the apostle Paul in 2 Corinthians 4:6: "For God, who commanded the light to shine out of darkness, hath shined in our hearts, to give the light of the knowledge of the glory of God in the face of Jesus Christ." When we accept Christ, the Light of the world, as Savior by inviting Him into our hearts, and we let Him anoint our eyes, then our spiritual eyes are opened, just like the blind man, and we are able to see.

DRY BONES AND SPIRITUAL BONE MARROW FAILURE

Ezekiel 37:1–10 relates the story of Ezekiel in the valley of the dry bones. Verse 11 reveals to us that these bones actually speak of the nation of Israel and its restoration, but I would like to use this example of the dry bones and their healing and apply it to us as individuals and to the church as the body of Christ. I will explain what it means physically and spiritually to have dry bones.

The Spirit of the Lord carried Ezekiel into the midst of the valley, which was filled with dry bones, and the latter part of verse 2 exclaims, "...lo, they were *very* dry" (emphasis mine). These bones represented a body that was once living and moist and joined together, but dried up and fell apart. The vultures, worms, and other animals had cleaned off all the tissue (the muscles, tendons, and ligaments) from the bones, and the bone marrow dried up as the heat of the sun evaporated any remaining moisture. They had obviously been dead for a long time and were seemingly beyond hope of living again as far as the natural is concerned.

Bones are usually very moist, having an abundant blood supply, and they are filled with an amazing substance called marrow. Surprisingly this is described in Job 21:24: "...his bones are moistened with marrow." The marrow not only contains blood cells, but it also stores iron and other building supplies necessary to continually form new cells as the old ones die off or are lost through trauma or other bleeding.

Bone marrow produces all the cells present in the blood and is located in the center of the bone. It is basically a factory that manufactures the immature forms of blood cells, called stem cells. The body then sends signals to the bone marrow to trigger these cells to mature and be released into the bloodstream as they are needed. The three basic types of blood cells (a trinity) that the body requires include red cells, white cells, and platelets. The red cells carry the oxygen in the blood to all the other cells in the body. White cells are part of the immune system that help fight off infection, and platelets are necessary to help form clots and control bleeding in case of injury. Healthy bone marrow (moist bone) is therefore necessary for life. If the bone marrow dries up and fails to produce adequate numbers of any of these cells, a person would soon die.

When a person is sick, a doctor usually orders a test called a CBC (Complete Blood Count), which measures the numbers of these three cell types. If the numbers are very low, then it may be necessary to do a bone marrow biopsy to try to determine the cause. For this test a doctor must take a special needle called a "Jamshidi" needle to drill through the outer bone into the core to obtain a sample of marrow for analysis. This needle is sharp on two edges and hollow in the middle and very strong. In cases of severe trauma or serious illness resulting in shock, in which fluids must be infused rapidly into the body, a similar needle called an intraosseous needle can be forced into the center of the bone, where the bone marrow is located, to deliver those fluids. This allows a large amount of fluid to be infused in a short period of time.

In Proverbs 17:22, we read that "a merry heart doeth good like a medicine: but a broken spirit drieth the bones [the bone marrow]." Proverbs 3:8 tells us that the fear of the Lord is "...health to thy navel, and marrow to thy bones." We know this to be true medically, as depression and extreme stress can actually alter the number of white cells that your bone marrow produces. The nation of Israel lost their fear of the Lord and began to serve the gods of the nations surrounding them. They no longer had a merry heart (the joy of the Lord), and their bone marrow began to dry up. If we fail to put God first in our hearts and allow the cares of this life to take priority, we will soon dry up and become lifeless, no longer able to stand against Satan.

In Ezekiel 37:3, God asks Ezekiel, "...can these bones live?" The answer is found in verse 4 as God tells Ezekiel to speak to the bones and say, "...O ye dry bones, hear the word of the LORD." The Word of God has the power to give or restore life. It is "...quick, [living] and powerful, and sharper than any twoedged sword, piercing even to the dividing asunder of soul and spirit, and of the joints and marrow..." (Heb. 4:12). It is like the sharp, two-edged intraosseous needle that can pierce into the marrow and infuse life into someone who is dying. The Word of His grace gives resurrection power to those who yield to its cutting and piercing of the soul. It is able to both diagnose and bring healing for spiritual bone marrow failure.

In a living body, the bones are held together by joints, connected by ligaments, and surrounded by muscles attached by the tendons, to allow movement, enabling the body to function. The dry bones in the valley not only needed to be moistened with marrow, but they needed to be joined together as a body and then to be given breath. This is promised in Ezekiel 37:6: "And I will lay sinews upon you, and will bring flesh upon you, and cover you with skin, and put breath in you, and ye shall live...."

This can only be accomplished by the life-giving Word of God's grace, which is able to build us up (Acts 20:32). Ephesians 4:15–16 shows us how this takes place: "But speaking the truth in love, may grow up into him in all things, which is the head, even Christ: From whom the whole body fitly joined together [with all the ligaments and tendons] and compacted by that which every joint supplieth...." The Word of God *pulls us together* as a body and *builds us up* in order so that we may stand in this evil day.

But to have life we must have breath, even as Ezekiel's dry bones in the valley. In Ezekiel 37:7–8, Ezekiel prophesied (spoke God's Word): "...and the bones came together...." However, "...there was no breath in them." Then in verse 10, God commanded Ezekiel to prophesy to the wind, "...and the breath came into them, and they lived, and stood upon their feet, an exceeding great army."

Second Tim. 3:16 declares, "All scripture is given by inspiration of God [God breathed]...." In the physical body, inspiration is part of the breathing process and means "to inhale or take a breath." God's breath (His Word) gives life. God's Word is breathed into us by the Holy Spirit, causing it to become real and living in our hearts, not just words on paper. God literally breathes into our souls the breath of life, as He did into Adam's physical body, through His Word. We can then breathe out God's Word by the power of the Holy Spirit to give life to someone else.

Does your life seem to be falling apart, and you just can't seem to get it back together? Are you drying up and suffering from spiritual bone marrow failure? Do you no longer have a merry heart? Are you lacking the joy of the Lord? Let the Word of God penetrate your dried-up bones and fill them with life-giving marrow, and allow the Holy Spirit to quicken the Word to your heart. His grace will build you up and give you strength to stand.

Yes, those dry bones can live again!

HAVE YOU BEEN IN THE SUN?

Someone once asked me if I had been in the sun, and I thought, "Well, it's kind of obvious, isn't it? I have a tan, right? So, that means I've been in the sun, right?" Maybe, maybe not. There are, in fact, "fake bakes," or tanning beds, so it is not necessarily strange to be asked if you have been in the sun when you have a tan. The point is that just because you *look* like you have been in the sun may not mean that you really have been. Perhaps it is only an artificial tan.

In this chapter, I am going to discuss the benefits and hazards of being in the sun and what it means spiritually. Life cannot exist without sunlight. If you plant a tomato under a tree, it may grow, but it will not bear fruit because of the shade. Likewise, the human body requires sunlight for optimal health, and we require spiritual sunlight to bear fruit. Exposure to the sun will soon produce outward evidence, as you will either develop a tan or a sunburn. But there are also important things that take place on the inside that eventually become apparent on the outside. If you completely avoid the sun, not only will you not get a tan, but you may also become depressed and weak. Thus, it is advantageous to spend time in the sun.

Just as light is necessary for physical life, so it is for spiritual life. John 1:1–2 and 4 states, "In the beginning was the Word, and the Word was with God, and the Word was God. The same was in the beginning with God. In him was life; and the life was the light of men." So, here it is: Jesus is the Word, and He is the Life and the Light; these are interchangeable. "That was the true Light [Jesus], which lighteth every man that cometh into the world" (John 1:9).

Not everyone receives that Light, the Light that was shown into the world when it was without form and void (Gen. 1:2–3). Darkness was upon the face of the deep, but God shined His light in the darkness. He also shines the "glorious light of the gospel" (2 Cor. 4:4) to everyone who will receive it, through Jesus Christ. Malachi prophesied of that Light in Malachi 4:2: "But unto you that fear my name shall the Sun of righteousness arise with healing in his wings." Jesus in this verse is called the Sun, which brings healing for both the body and the soul. Without Him there is no life, physical or spiritual.

I think it is interesting that most of the Scriptures related to the Light of the world are found in John's gospel and in his epistle, 1 John. Perhaps it is because he leaned on Jesus' breast and was intimately acquainted with that Light.

Jesus said in John 8:12: "I am the light of the world: he that followeth me shall not walk in darkness, but shall have the light of life." In John 11:9–10, He further declares, "Are there not twelve hours in the day? If any man walk in the day he stumbleth not, because he seeth the light of this world. But if a man walk in the night, he stumbleth, because there is no light in him." This is, of course, speaking of Jesus, the true Light, without whom we are all in darkness. Vitamin D, often called the sunshine vitamin, is an extremely important hormone that has been studied extensively in the past few years. We obtain vitamin D mostly from fortified foods and from the sun. Exposure to sunlight causes a chemical reaction to take place in the skin that produces vitamin D. Every organ system in the body has been discovered to have vitamin D receptors, indicating its necessity to the entire body. Vitamin D has been shown to decrease the risk of breast and colon cancer, to help prevent Parkinson's disease and diabetes, and to reduce the risk of heart disease and heart failure by about 50 percent.

Tanning booths produce a tan, but they do not trigger the production of vitamin D in the skin. Because of this, the incidence of melanoma, a potentially deadly skin cancer, from tanning booths is three times that of exposure to natural sunlight. The sun through vitamin D production can help protect you from cancer as long as you do not get a sunburn.

In order to produce adequate vitamin D from the sunlight, a person needs ten to fifteen minutes of unprotected exposure daily (without sunscreen). Likewise, the spiritual man requires daily exposure to the Light of the Word. Do you know how hard it is to get ten to fifteen minutes of time in the Word without interruption? It is about as difficult as getting ten to fifteen minutes of unprotected sunlight.

Satan does not want us to have more light shined into our hearts and lives, so he will do everything possible to distract as from reading God's Word. We just can't seem to fit it into our busy schedule, or we receive phone calls or interruptions from children or other family or friends. Perhaps even our daily chores seem to take precedence over Bible reading.

The more light we receive, the more we understand, for the entrance of His Word gives light (Ps. 119:30). We can walk in the light, because we have the Word as a lamp unto our feet and a light unto our path (Ps. 119:105). Ephesians 5:8 advises us, "For ye were sometimes [at one time] darkness, but now are ye light in the Lord: walk as children of light." Walk in the Light, and you will receive the vitamin D from the *Son*. Both the *Son* and the *sun* give life and light to keep you from falling.

Sunlight also helps depression. Sunlight enters into the brain through the pupils of your eyes, striking the retina, and is transmitted into the pituitary gland situated behind the eyes, which stimulates the production of serotonin, the body's natural antidepressant. This only occurs with full spectrum light such as sunlight.

Depression can actually be induced by confining someone to a dark place for a prolonged period of time, thereby depleting their serotonin. There are parts of the world that receive less sunlight, and the people who live there are more prone to depression. During the winter months, a certain type of depression may occur due to shortened days with decrease in sunlight. This is called S.A.D., or Seasonal Affective Disorder. Spending most of our time under artificial lighting with little exposure to the sun or full spectrum lighting could also be responsible for the epidemic of depression present in the United States today.

If we have adequate exposure to the true *Son light* of the Word of God, He will give us the joy of salvation, for which David prayed in Psalm 51:12. Ecclesiastes 11:7 declares, "Truly the light is sweet and a pleasant thing it is for the eyes to behold the sun." Both natural and spiritual light will therefore benefit depression. However, the Scripture tells us that the nature of mankind is to turn his face from the light. In Isaiah 53:3, we read concerning Jesus, "He is despised and rejected of men; a man of sorrows, and acquainted with grief: and we hid as it were our faces from him."

As a whole, the religious world today is rejecting the true Light of the gospel, as in John 3:19: "And this is the condemnation, that light is come into the world, and men loved darkness rather than light, because their deeds were evil." They have a form of godliness but deny the power thereof (2 Tim. 3:15), having as it were a tanning booth religion. In other words, they want to appear as if they have been in the *Son*, but they have never been exposed to the Light of God's Word. They preach a man-made, artificial Son light, fake gospel that does not lift up the name of Jesus or glorify God. It only glorifies and lifts up man to make man look better. However, we cannot have life without the true Light. Likewise, artificial light does not produce the vitamin D that is needed for life.

Now, what about overexposure to sunlight? There is necessity of sunlight, but we must avoid overexposure. So, how do we do that? In the natural you can use sunscreen, wear a hat, wear long sleeves, or carry an umbrella to protect yourself. Overexposure will cause sunburn, and repeated sunburn can lead to skin cancer, so protection is vital.

There are spiritual dangers also to overexposure. David declares in Psalm 84:11: "For the LORD God is a sun and shield: the LORD will give grace and glory...." Not only is He our Sun but He shields us from the Sun. Exposure to the judgment of God, like the midday sun, without any covering will cause severe burning. God shows up our sin through the light of the gospel, revealing to us that we are all sinners, and therefore under condemnation and the sentence of death. If all He did was expose our sin, we would experience overexposure to the Sun with burning. (However, underexposure to the Sun will also cause burning—in hell!)

God has made our physical body in a unique way that helps protect us from burning. We have special cells on our skin called melanocytes. These are the cells that give skin its color. Some people genetically have more to begin with and thus their skin is darker. Others are rather unlucky, and their skin is extremely light, allowing them to burn easily. But even a light-skinned person should get at least ten minutes of unprotected sun exposure every day. The sun itself triggers the melanocytes to release a pigment called melanin, which turns the skin darker, resulting in a tan. That darkness then acts as an umbrella, or a shield.

There is an average of sixty-thousand melanocytes per square inch of your skin, which work to help protect us from overexposure to the sun. The Lord God is a Sun because He is the Light, but He is also a Shield, for He gives grace, which acts like the melanocytes to protect us from His wrath. The more Sun exposure, the more grace He gives.

We also see this in Psalm 121:5–6: "...the LORD is thy shade upon thy right hand. The sun shall not smite thee by day...." God's wrath, like the burning sun in the middle of the desert, would cause severe burning in a short period of time if there were no covering.

All men are naked before Him and exposed. Our righteousness is as filthy rags, so we would have no covering if it were not for His grace to protect us from judgment. God, through His infinite love and mercy, has provided the Son, the Sun of righteousness, the Light, who was the Word, full of grace and truth. We are fully protected for He is also our Shield, to come between us and the wrath of God.

In summary, if we have been walking in the Light, there should be outward evidence manifested for the world to see (i.e., our spiritual suntan). It will be the direct result of exposure to the true Light, not as a result of our own self effort. No artificial tan or "fake bakes" are accepted! In addition, we will be able to walk in His strength without falling. Our lives will also show forth the joy of the Lord as the Son-light raises our spiritual serotonin levels.

Have you been in the Son today?

SPIRITUAL DIGESTION: EATING THE BREAD OF LIFE

I am going to discuss the physical process of digestion and compare it to eating the Bread of Life. Jesus, in John 6, was speaking to the Pharisees along with others in the crowd regarding the eating of His flesh. Many were offended, as they did not understand the spiritual meaning of His words. In verses 48–49, He declared, "I am that bread of life. Your fathers did eat manna in the wilderness, and are dead." He explained to them that the bread that Moses gave, which God sent down from heaven, did not really bring life because the people still died in the wilderness. However, He proclaimed in verse 50: "This is the bread which cometh down from heaven, that a man may eat thereof, and not die." I can just imagine Him speaking to them, then pointing to Himself and saying, "This is the bread that came down from heaven " (v. 50), and "I am the living bread which came down from heaven: if any man eat of this bread, he shall live forever: and the bread that I will give is my flesh, which I will give for the life of the world. The Jews therefore strove among themselves, saying, How can this man give us his flesh to eat?" (vv. 51–52). That sounded repulsive to them, and it would be to you, too, if you were thinking only in the natural. "Then

Jesus said unto them, Verily, verily, I say unto you, Except ye eat the flesh of the Son of man, and drink his blood, ye have no life in you" (v. 53).

According to the Law, they were strictly forbidden to drink any blood, and to think of eating another man's flesh would, indeed, be repulsive to them. "Whoso eateth my flesh, and drinketh my blood, hath eternal life; and I will raise him up at the last day. For my flesh is meat indeed, and my blood is drink indeed. He that eateth my flesh, and drinketh my blood, dwelleth in me, and I in him" (vv. 54–56). The question is, how can we eat His flesh and drink His blood? How can we do that?

First of all, I will tell you what this is not. We are not talking about communion, eating the bread and drinking the wine. That is a commemorative service in which we remember what Jesus did for us when He gave His life on the cross. The text here is about something far more personal, something we should do every day, just as we must eat every day.

We pray, "Give us this day our daily bread" (Matt. 6:11). We need our daily bread physically and spiritually, but what is that bread from heaven? John 1:1 declares that, "In the beginning was the Word, and the Word was with God, and the Word was God." Then we read in verse 14: "And the Word was made flesh, and dwelt among us…." Jesus was the Word, and He was made flesh in order that He could dwell among us and die for us. We are to eat His flesh, meaning that we eat the Word and let it become a part of us.

When you eat bread physically, it becomes a part of you; you are what you eat. What goes in your mouth literally becomes a part of you. Whatever you eat is absorbed into your body, into your bloodstream, and it becomes the proteins in your body and the things that your body needs, what the cells in your body require in order to grow and function. So, what you feed your physical body is what your body will end up looking like. We are what we eat in the natural, and we are also what we eat in the spiritual.

I am going to discuss the physical act of eating food, from the beginning to the end, and how it is digested into our system. I will define the many steps along the way in a simplified manner in order to show what it means to us spiritually to eat the Bread of Life. The digestive tract has a beginning (the mouth) and an ending (at the rectal sphincter). So, food goes in one end and out the other, but there are important processes that take place in between whereby the body absorbs important nutrients and eliminates the waste products. All of this has a spiritual meaning as you will soon see.

Digestion begins in the mouth, where your body produces saliva containing enzymes that break down carbohydrates—that is, the sweet things and foods that metabolize into sugar. In addition to that, saliva moistens the food so it won't go down dry.

In fact, digestion really begins before you even put the food in your mouth. When you begin to smell food cooking, your saliva will begin to flow to be ready to digest your food. Even the stomach juices begin to flow in preparation for this. You can liken that to the spiritual, for when you go to church and begin to sing songs, you may become hungry in anticipation of being fed the Word of God.

The food first touches the tongue, which enables you to taste. The tongue is also a muscle. This is necessary because as you chew your food, it pushes it back and forth between the teeth to break it down into small enough portions to swallow it.

We are to "…taste and see that the Lord is good…" (Ps. 34:8). Psalm 119:103 likewise declares, "How sweet are thy words unto my taste! yea, sweeter than honey to my mouth." So, when the food enters our mouth and we taste it with our tongue, moistening it with saliva, digestion of the carbohydrates has already begun.

Teeth are necessary for digestion in order to break down food into smaller particles. A person cannot just shove food into his mouth and hope to be able to swallow it, or I may need to perform the Heimlich maneuver on him, and that which went into the mouth would come back out again. The food would do him no good at all. It is absolutely necessary to get the food from the mouth down into the stomach. Thus, we must also chew the Word of God, and that requires teeth. We see a beautiful example of their necessity in Song of Songs 4:2, where the Bridegroom says to the bride, "Thy teeth are like a flock of sheep…." We first note that there are a flock of them, not just one, and they are, "…even shorn…." They are healthy, well-developed teeth, "…which came up from the washing…," indicating cleanliness. He continues with, "…whereof every one bear twins…," and "…none is barren among them." There are no missing teeth, plenty of teeth with which to chew the Word of God.

The Word that you receive at church must be taken home with you so that you can chew on it in order to receive the full benefit of it. This means to meditate on it, as in Psalm 1:2 with your spiritual teeth.

Eating implies swallowing. We don't just put food in our mouth, taste it, and then spit it out. Sadly, there are people who have heard the Word of God and tasted it, and yet that is as far as it goes, because they don't chew it and swallow it and allow it to become a part of them. Jesus said in Revelation 3:16, "...because thou art lukewarm, and neither cold nor hot, I will spue thee out of my mouth," indicating that those to whom He was speaking did not become a part of Him. When we eat, we must swallow in order to benefit from the food.

When we swallow, the food goes straight down to the stomach through the esophagus. The food then encounters digestive juices, mainly hydrochloric acid, to break it down even further. The stomach, also being a muscle, begins to contract and mix the food with the acid. In order for food to be absorbed into your body, it must be converted into a liquid state. Stomach acid is required for that process and should not be completely eliminated.

Before I go further into that, let us examine some Scriptures regarding eating and swallowing the Word of God. "And I went unto the angel, and said unto him, Give me the little book. And he said unto me, Take it, and eat it up; and it shall make thy belly bitter, but it shall be in thy mouth sweet as honey" (Rev. 10:9). We read earlier that the Word of God is sweeter than honey to the taste (that is in the mouth, where the taste occurs). Food then goes from the mouth to the stomach, and then it becomes bitter (because of the acid). In verse 10, we read, "And I took the little book out of the angel's hand, and ate it up; and it was in my mouth sweet as honey: and as soon as I had eaten it, my belly was bitter."

The prophet declares in Jeremiah 15:16: "Thy words were found, and I did eat them; and thy word was unto me the joy and rejoicing of mine heart...." First of all, you must *seek* the Word in order to find it; you must be desirous and hungry for the Word of God. Today there is a famine for the hearing of the Word; people do not want to hear it. You will not eat if you are not hungry.

Like Jeremiah, we must eat the Word, swallow it, and let it mix with the acid. If you have ever had acid reflux, you know how bitter that acid is. However, that acid is necessary. Remember that I am a physician, and one of the mistakes that doctors make is trying to interfere too much with "mother nature" (we know that is actually a reference to God). God put that acid in the stomach for a purpose, because it is necessary for the absorption of many minerals and to break down proteins in your food. We prescribe medications that decrease the acid to provide symptom relief and help heal ulcers. The little purple pill that takes away all the acid makes you feel good, but it can have side effects, if taken long-term. If you are on medications called proton pump inhibitors, such as Prilosec or Nexium, that completely suppress acid, be aware that they could also increase your risk of heart disease, stroke, anemia, and even kidney failure. You should talk to your doctor about not staying on these medications long-term or being on the lowest possible dose for your condition.

Some churches will try to eliminate the bitterness of the Word of God, but the acid is necessary. We not only need the sweet promises, but the rod of His correction if we are to grow, even if the chastening is not pleasant. The Word of God must be applied personally in spite of the bitterness.

There are times in your life when the trials are hot and burning, just like the acid. The Lord may give you a little temporary relief, but He will not take you out of that trial until He is finished working His Word in you. If you really want to grow spiritually, you must stay in the acid. Jonah found that out when he was literally in the acid of the whale's belly for three days.

The apostle Paul seemed to encounter a similar situation with the acid when he asked God to remove something that he termed a "thorn in the flesh..." (2 Cor. 12:7). He did not specifically define what the thorn was in order that we could apply it to our own situation. He prayed earnestly three times, which reminds us of Jesus, who also prayed three times for His bitter cup to pass from Him. God's answer to Paul was in essence, "No, I have a purpose in it." But "...my grace is sufficient for thee: for my strength is made perfect in weakness..." (2 Cor. 12:9).

Trials are necessary for our growth in the Lord. Rather than pray for the Lord to take them away, we should pray for Him to enable us to grow through them. We grow as we assimilate His Word, for it is the Word of His grace, which is able to build us up. If we do not go through trials, then we will never fully understand and appreciate His grace. He gives more grace when the trials are hotter. Where more acid prevails, He pours in more grace to endure it.

Thus far, we have discussed the journey from the mouth to the stomach, which is now churning and tossing the food back and forth, mixing it up, similar to what the disciples experienced when they were tossed about by the winds in the storm. This is what happens to us when we are in the stomach experience. We know that the Word of God is working in our lives, but we may wonder, "Wow, I don't know how long this is going to go on!" Be of good cheer—there is an outlet in the stomach!

While it was a straight shot from the mouth to the stomach, the rest of the digestive tract is no longer a straight tube anymore. The stomach takes a little curve, and then we enter the small intestine. The small intestine then winds back and forth multiple times for about fifteen or twenty feet. You may think, "Well, if I were designing this thing, I would make it shorter. Why should you have to go through all of that twisting and turning?" I will tell you what would happen if it was shorter and straighter. It is the same thing that happens to people if they have had intestinal surgery due to cancer or other problem requiring part of the bowel to be removed. They develop a condition called "short bowel syndrome," where the food passes through too quickly without enough time to absorb it, resulting in constant diarrhea. They lose weight due to malabsorption of their nutrients.

We may find ourselves asking, "Lord, when is this trial going to end? How long is it going to take?" The time that it takes to go through your system is the time that it takes to work the Word in your life. His timing is perfect, always perfect, as He has a purpose in that.

Inside the small intestine there are many folds, and inside the lining of the small intestine are little "fingers," or "villi." If you examine them under a microscope, you will find there are even more little villi, like little straws (they are not really straws—I am just using that as an example). The villi will take the food, which is now liquified, and suck it in, absorbing it through the wall of the small intestine into the bloodstream. However, the liquified food must be slowed down by all of those folds in order to allow enough time for this to take place.

Scripture also refers to something with many folds in 1 Peter 4:10: "...the manifold grace of God." The grace of God has many folds (many aspects, many folds), for it is manifold. Whatever your situation in life is, whatever you are going through right now, it is enabling God to work His purpose in your life, to enable you to grow in Christ. If you want to be like Christ, then you must eat Him, that is the Word of God. It must not only be received, but absorbed, to become a part of you. If it just goes through quickly and is never absorbed, the Word will not be worked out in your life.

Paul stated that he gloried in tribulation, because when he was weak then he was strong. It is the trials, the tribulations, the many obstacles, the many folds in our lives, the curves and the detours, the things we do not like that are necessary for our full growth in Christ. Thus, we need to allow the Lord time to work in us through those trials and experience the manifold grace of God. Do not try to push things through by taking a laxative. The Word needs time to be absorbed. Don't rush God! And don't rush through the eating of His Word!

Jesus said that we are to eat His flesh and drink His blood. What does that mean, to "drink His blood"? Where is the life? The life is in the blood, right? So, when we drink His blood, we are partaking of His life. It is Christ in me. I must partake of His life, not just taste it, but eat it and let it actually become a part of me. I must eat the Word and drink His life.

We have now gone through the small intestine, and the body has absorbed all it can of the liquified food. I have purposely not mentioned all of the other parts of digestion, such as the pancreas with its secretion of enzymes to break down the fats, or the gall bladder, which releases bile. I have rather concentrated on the absorption of nourishment through the digestive tract.

After absorption is complete, the waste products must be eliminated. The Old Testament city of Jerusalem had several gates, and one of them was called the Dung Gate. It was used for exactly what its name implies. People did not enter the city through that gate. It was only used to get rid of waste and was therefore a very necessary gate.

In the body, the colon collects all the unabsorbable food products, the waste material and fiber. Everything that cannot be absorbed and utilized for your benefit must be eliminated. The colon, or large intestine, reabsorbs all the extra water so the waste material can begin to take shape, to have a form. The waste is collected, stored, formed, and processed for the sole purpose of eliminating it. If you do not expel it, you are going to be pretty miserable and would soon have a bowel obstruction. You certainly do not want a physical or a spiritual bowel obstruction. Ideally, waste should be eliminated on a daily basis to maintain good health.

But how does this apply to us spiritually? This is a necessary part of growing in grace, not just eating the Bread of Life, but eliminating that which is detrimental to our spiritual man. Paul mentioned a spiritual "Dung Gate" in Philippians

3:7–8, when he declared, "But what things were gain to me, [those things that I thought were good] those I counted loss for Christ. Yea, doubtless, and I count all things but loss for the excellency of the knowledge of Christ Jesus my Lord… and do count them but dung that I may win Christ." That means all the things of this world that inhibit our growth in Christ. Those things that we think to be good may actually hinder us. We must collect and get rid of everything in our lives that is not pleasing to the Lord. Things that please the flesh must be eliminated in order to maintain spiritual health and grow up into Christ in all things.

I will summarize by saying that eating the Bread of Life begins in the mouth. We taste the sweetness of the Word but find that it may result in bitter trials as the Lord works in our lives. We then allow God time to accomplish His purpose in us, to enable us to become more like Him through His manifold grace. We partake of His blood, His very life, and we meditate on His Word daily. We must also allow Him to sort out the things in our lives that would be detrimental. We count them as dung, as did Paul, to be emptied out in order that we may take in more of the Word of God and grow in grace.

SPIRITUAL DEHYDRATION

Dehydration can be serious or life-threatening, and it results from failure or the inability to take in enough water to replace fluid that is lost through work, exposure to heat, illness, or injury. The body has only a limited supply of water stored up. It can store a lot of fat but only enough water to last a few days, up to two weeks, depending on the environment. You can go a long time without food but not without water, even though water makes up about 70 percent of your body weight.

Water in the Bible is a picture of the Word, the Holy Spirit and Christ. It is extremely important both physically and spiritually and it must be pure. There is no substitute for water. Sports drinks and sugary drinks, including juice, are too concentrated and do not quench thirst. They can actually cause a dehydrated person to become more dehydrated if they are used in place of water for hydration.

The Word and the Spirit work together, for it is the Holy Spirit who makes God's Word real to us. We need the Word spiritually as much as we need water physically, and there is no substitute for the pure Word of God.

I am going to discuss the importance of water to the physical body and the mechanisms that the body uses to try to avoid dehydration. This will in turn help you to understand the necessity of partaking of the Living Water for the soul.

Most of the time we do not drink enough water even when we are thirsty. We just drink enough to take away the dryness in our mouth. So how do we know if we are getting dehydrated, both physically and spiritually? What are some of the signs and symptoms?

When you first start getting dehydrated, your urine will turn darker and more concentrated and you go less often in smaller amounts. You may also begin to feel lightheaded and weak, with difficulty standing or walking. Severe dehydration can cause confusion and lethargy. Spiritually we would also have difficulty standing against Satan or running the race. We would be too weak to put on our spiritual armor, as described in Ephesians 6:13–17 to fight our spiritual warfare.

In order to diagnose a small child or infant with dehydration, prior to being able to obtain blood or urine tests, a doctor looks for dry mucous membranes in the mouth. But one of the most important signs we look for is that when the child cries, there are no tears. The tears dry up because the body is trying to conserve fluid.

Tears are also important spiritually, for a lack of them is a sign of spiritual dehydration. Do you weep for lost souls? Are you able to feel the pain of a brother or sister in Christ and weep for them or with them instead of condemning them? Jesus wept, and we should too. We are instructed in Romans 12:15 to "rejoice with them that do rejoice, and weep with them that weep." Hebrews 4:15 tells us that Jesus, our High Priest, is touched by the feeling of our infirmities, which means that He weeps along with us. David knew that his tears were important to God and that none of them were wasted, for he asked God in Psalm 56:8: "put thou my tears into thy bottle." If your eyes are not able to shed tears, then you may be spiritually dehydrated and in need of more Living Water.

When Jesus was on the cross, He manifested three important signs of dehydration that occurred because of fluid loss that he was not able to replace: thirst, weakness, and dry mouth. In John 19:28 He cried out, "I thirst," and they offered Him vinegar to drink, but He refused it. The severely dehydrated state of shock resulting from crucifixion was prophesied in Psalm 22:15, in which the Messiah was to utter, "My strength is dried up...my tongue cleaveth to my jaws." This statement indicated a mouth that was so dry that His tongue stuck to the roof of His mouth and also that He experienced extreme weakness. Jesus, the One who is the Living Water, poured out His life and suffered thirst and weakness in order to give us His strength and an unending supply of the Water of life to quench our thirsty souls.

Daily water intake is necessary for three major processes in our body: for purifying or cleansing, for cooling, and for our electrical system. Our bodies run on electricity, which requires a flow of positive and negative ions to generate a current. These ions, such as sodium, chloride, and potassium, also called electrolytes, must be dissolved in water and must be at the proper concentration at all times. Our kidneys help to regulate this, but adequate water intake is necessary in order to do that. The average American diet is too high in sodium (salt). Also, there is a high consumption of soda pop and sports drinks, which contain large amounts of it and must be flushed out with water or they can be harmful.

The Holy Spirit was promised by Jesus in John 7:38–39, in which He was typified as rivers of living water. But the

Spirit is also the source of power (the electrical system) for the Christian. Jesus offers us this power in Acts 1:8: "But ye shall receive power, after that the Holy Ghost is come upon you: and ye shall be witnesses unto me." Not only does the Holy Spirit flow through us like a current of electricity to empower us to witness, but He enables us to have power over Satan and provides the power to walk in the Spirit so we will not fulfill the lust of the flesh (Gal. 5:16). As a result, we can be assured, "That the righteousness of the law might be fulfilled *in* us [not *by* us], who walk not after the flesh, but after the Spirit" (Rom. 8:4). In addition, the Holy Spirit gives us the power to comprehend the riches and hidden treasures in God's Word and promises to lead us into all truth, as much as our thirsty souls desire.

Besides helping to regulate our electrolytes, the kidneys help to filter and cleanse our body as the blood flows through them. Waste products from metabolism are produced daily and must be flushed out or they will poison us. Also, the breakdown products of certain medications are filtered out and eliminated through this flushing as we drink water.

Spiritually it is the water of the Word that cleanses us, and it should be partaken of regularly to allow this to happen. "Where withal [how] shall a young man [or woman] cleanse his way? By taking heed thereto according to thy word" (Ps. 119:9). The apostle Paul tells us in Ephesians 5:25–26 that Christ loved the church and gave Himself for it in order "that he [Christ] might sanctify and cleanse it [the church] with the washing of the water by the word." The Word of God cleanses us of the impurities that accumulate in our daily walk with the Lord while in this body of flesh. We cannot cleanse ourselves. Christ died in order that He might do the cleansing for us, much like He did when He washed His disciples' feet. All we need to do is to drink in the Word daily and allow the cleansing to take place. The kidneys cannot do the flushing and cleansing of the natural body without water. Likewise, our spirit relies on the Word to purify us.

The third important process for which the body requires water is for cooling. The body utilizes an evaporative cooling system to help regulate body temperature. If you are running or working hard, you will soon start sweating. The sweat then evaporates, taking the heat with it. This may happen on a hot day even at rest. Cars and some machines also use water as a cooling system to avoid overheating and damage.

Long distance runners must take in more water than they think they need, due to evaporation and fluid loss, in order to avoid dehydration and muscle cramps. They cannot store up water ahead of time, so they continue to drink as they run. The same is true spiritually. We are running to win Christ as Bridegroom (not for salvation, which has already been bought). We must keep drinking the water of the Word as we continue running so that we will not faint. If we are going to be able to run and not be weary (Is. 40:30), we cannot allow ourselves to get spiritually dehydrated.

Heat stroke can occur if you are in the sun or extreme heat and fail to drink enough water to sweat. The body temperature will rise to a dangerous level because the body is unable to cool itself. You must drink extra water to avoid this. Only water, no other fluids, can prevent heat stroke. The same thing is true spiritually. Jesus said to the woman at the well in John 4:10 that He was the Living Water and that only He could satisfy her thirst and meet her needs.

We also need to take in more water when we are in the heat of trials. If we drink enough of the Living Water, we will even be able to stand the heat of the fiery furnace. We see in Daniel 3:17–25 that the three Hebrew captives, Shadrach, Meshach, and Abed-nego, were able to withstand the fire because they had an inexhaustible water supply with them in the midst of their fiery trial (v. 25). Jesus has also promised to be with *us* through any trials and to make a way of escape (1 Cor. 10:13). That way of escape is through the water of the Word, the Holy Spirit and the Living Water, whereby the overcomers "quenched the violence of fire" (Heb. 11:34).

God has designed our bodies to have a special regulatory system in order to help prevent dehydration. It involves the coordination of the brain and the kidneys. The kidneys regulate how much water is eliminated through the urine based on the concentration of the blood. If there is too much sodium in your blood due to consuming excess salt from your diet or soda pop and sports drinks, then the kidneys will try to dilute that down by holding on to the body's water. The same thing happens if we do not drink enough water, which causes the blood to become more concentrated. This results in urine that is darker yellow, since it is more concentrated, to conserve water loss. Dark urine is a sign that you are not drinking enough water. A doctor can do a urine test to check the kidneys and see if you are dehydrated.

The Lord also does a spiritual kidney test on us to see if we are drinking enough Living Water. David said in Psalm 26:2: "Examine me, O LORD, and prove me; try my reins and my heart." The "reins" are the kidneys and refer to our innermost being. Doctors use a similar word, "renal," when speaking of the kidneys. The Lord is able to try (test) our "heart and reins" to see if we are in need of spending more time at the feet of Jesus and drinking in the water of the Word as did Mary in the story of Mary and Martha in Luke 10:38–42.

The brain, in addition to the kidneys, monitors the concentration of the blood and the electrolytes for the purpose of triggering the thirst mechanism to cause us to drink more water if needed. Doctors no longer think there is a specific thirst center in the brain because it is so complex, involving not only the hypothalamus but other parts of the brain as well. The hypothalamus receives input from sensors in blood vessels that monitor the thickness of the blood and the blood pressure. If the blood concentration is too high, a signal is sent to tell you to drink more water to dilute it back down. Even small changes of 1 or 2 percent in the concentration will trigger thirst. In addition to this, when the body gets too low in water, the pituitary gland releases a hormone called vasopressin, or antidiuretic hormone, which signals the kidneys to decrease urine output and conserve water. Both the brain and the kidneys will then release a combination of hormones that result in the sensation of thirst.

Thirst is necessary for survival. By the time you feel thirsty, you are already partially dehydrated. The body tells you to drink water, but too often people will try to quench their thirst with fluids that contain sugar or salt, which only compounds the problem.

Since water is also necessary for life spiritually, our soul has been given a thirst for God. Jesus said, "If any man thirst, let him come unto me and drink" (John 7:37). Jesus Himself thirsted because He was in a body of flesh, as we see in John 4:7, when He asked the Samaritan woman for a drink of water. He met the woman at the well when she had come to draw water for her physical needs. But Jesus knew her heart and that she was also thirsty spiritually. However, she was thirsting for all the wrong things, and nothing satisfied her. She had already had five husbands and was living with a sixth man. She had a misguided thirst mechanism. So, Jesus offered her, and she accepted, the Living Water, which was able to quench her thirst.

People today are searching for the wrong things to satisfy their thirst: possessions, drugs, fame, sexual relationships, or anything that makes them feel better. It is like trying to quench physical thirst with water substitutes; it just doesn't work. Nothing can satisfy the thirsty soul except Jesus, the Water of Life. So, let us drink freely from the Living Water and avoid spiritual dehydration.

SPIRITUAL INCONTINENCE

Due to our rapidly aging population, including approximately 77 million baby boomers, and the problems that come with aging, we are beginning to see an increasing number of advertisements for urinary incontinence products. While this may be an important physical issue, incontinence is equally relevant spiritually, as I will explain. Incontinence can also refer to loss of bowel control or oral secretions (drooling).

The definition of *incontinence* is "without self-restraint, lack of self-control, incapable of containing, holding or keeping." This definition applies both physically and spiritually.

King Solomon in his wisdom describes in poetic form in Ecclesiastes 12:1–7 the process of aging in the physical body, illustrating the various functions that are affected. In verse 6 he refers to bladder incontinence by using the example of a cistern, which was common in those days, and the valve that controls the flow of water to be released, calling it "...the wheel broken at the cistern."

A cistern is a large receptacle or reservoir for storing water. In anatomy, a cistern is a sac or cavity containing natural fluid in the body. The bladder is therefore a cistern that catches and stores the water that drains into it from the kidneys until the appropriate time for it to be released. So, if the wheel was broken at the cistern, there would be no way to control the flow. Perhaps King Solomon was beginning to suffer from incontinence himself!

The apostle Paul refers to spiritual incontinence in 2 Timothy 3:3. In this chapter, he is warning the young preacher, Timothy, regarding conditions that will prevail in the last days related to the evil behavior of mankind, describing them in verse 3 as men "without natural affection, trucebreakers, false accusers, *incontinent*, fierce, despisers of those that are good" (emphasis mine).

Conditions such as these are reported in the news media daily, including reports of murders, child abuse, rape, and mass shootings in churches and synagogues, all indicative of a lack of self-control and the inability to contain the emotions or control behavior.

Stricter gun control cannot solve the problem of lack of self-restraint. Neither can prison, social reform, anger management classes, or antipsychotic medications. That's because the problem originates in the unregenerate heart. According to Jeremiah 17:9, "The heart is deceitful above all things and desperately wicked...." So, you see, only God holds the cure for this spiritual malady. Salvation (transformation, not reformation) is the answer. However, even after we are born again, we may still struggle with spiritual incontinence, for Satan delights in tempting us to do things that soil our testimony.

Let us explore the physical condition further in order to better understand and treat the spiritual problem. The number-one cause of incontinence is simply a matter of immaturity. Babies have no control of their bladder, bowel, or saliva, but they become continent as they mature and are toilet trained. That's due to the fact that their muscles are weak and uncoordinated at first and require time to finish developing and to strengthen.

As babes in Christ, we lack the spiritual strength to have full victory over the flesh, and we need to feed upon the Word of God in order to "grow up into him in all things" (Eph. 4:15). In the beginning we may find ourselves repeatedly messing in our diaper, doing things that cause a stench in God's nostrils, and needing to cry out to our heavenly Father to clean us up. But God is faithful to do just that because He loves us. First John 1:9 states: "If we confess our sins, he is faithful and just to forgive us our sins, and to cleanse us from all unrighteousness."

In addition, babies will drool, as they have no ability to control what comes rolling out of their mouth. This uncontrolled drooling may manifest itself spiritually with such things as gossip; profanity; angry, hurtful words; or constantly putting other people down while lifting oneself up.

Oral incontinence was addressed in James 3:8: "But the tongue can no man tame…," and in verse 10: "Out of the same mouth proceedeth blessing and cursing. My brethren, these things ought not so to be." Only God can control the tongue. We have no power in ourselves to control the things that slip out of our mouth; therefore, we have all been spiritually incontinent regarding this matter.

However, praise the Lord, there is help available through the power of the Holy Spirit. Galatians 5:16 tells us, "Walk in the Spirit, and ye shall not fulfill the lust [strong desires] of the flesh." It doesn't mean that we won't have those desires but that we can avoid fulfilling them through His power. The

Holy Spirit can guard our lips, as David prayed for in Psalm 141:3: "Set a watch [guard], O LORD, before my mouth; keep the door of my lips." But we must be willing to yield to and walk in the Spirit in order for this to happen.

Physical urinary incontinence can occur in adults due to the weakening of the muscles of the perineum (pelvic floor) following pregnancy and childbirth, being overweight, or simply due to the aging process. The most common type is called stress incontinence, because it occurs when the sphincter muscles are stressed by such things as coughing, sneezing, lifting, or even laughing hard. While the muscles may do a good job holding back the urine under normal circumstances, the pressure of this stress overcomes the strength of the muscles that have become weakened and incontinence occurs.

We sometimes find this to be true spiritually. When we are faced with stressful or overwhelming circumstances, we may suddenly lose control and become angry and say or do things that bring shame or hurt to others and soil our Christian testimony.

The treatment for weakened muscles, physically or spiritually, is exercise. There are special exercises for physical incontinence called Kegel exercises that help to strengthen the sphincter muscles and may be of significant benefit. Your doctor can give you information regarding this. If this is not successful, there are medications or surgical procedures that may help.

Exercise is likewise important in the treatment of spiritual incontinence. But how can we do this? We are given these instructions in 1 Timothy 4:7: "But refuse profane and old wives' fables, and *exercise* thyself rather unto godliness."

Profane and old wives' fables refer to things that are not true and apply to any religious teaching that denies the virgin birth of Christ, or His death, burial, resurrection, and second coming. Jesus Himself is the Truth. It is only the "…word of his grace, which is able to build you up [strengthen you]…" (Acts 20:32). All other teaching is deemed profane and of no value and is to be avoided. Not only is it not beneficial, but it is detrimental and will weaken us.

Continence is our spiritual goal. Continence is the opposite of incontinence and is characterized by self-restraint. Another similar word used in the Scripture is *temperance*, which refers to self-restraint in conduct. Temperance (self-control) is part of the fruit of the Spirit listed in Galatians 5:22–23: "But the fruit of the Spirit is love, joy, peace, longsuffering, gentleness, goodness, faith, meekness, *temperance*: against such is no law."

Note that this is fruit, not works. Only mature trees bear fruit. The tree does not decide what type of fruit that it will bear; it cannot pick and choose. All of the fruit of the Spirit will be manifest in our lives as we walk in the Spirit and become mature Christians by being rooted and grounded in the truth of His Word.

In summary, just as it is every parent's goal that their adorable babies will grow up and mature to the point that they are potty trained and that they are no longer messing their pants and needing diaper changes, so it is our heavenly Father's desire that we become spiritually continent. He has provided adequate toilet training through His Word so that we can bring honor rather than disgrace to His name.

The grace of God does not give us a license to continue with our spiritual incontinence. In fact, the more we understand of His grace, the more we desire to please Him in order that our lives will become a sweet-smelling savor unto God. Grace teaches us to be more like Him, as we learn in Titus 2:11–12: "For the grace of God that bringeth salvation hath appeared to all men, Teaching us that denying ungodliness and worldly lusts, we should live soberly, righteously, and godly, in this present world."

That means no more spiritual diapers or "Depends"! Instead, we *depend* on the Lord.

REACH OUT AND
TOUCH SOMEONE

Are you old enough to recall the old Bell Telephone advertisement, "Reach out and touch someone"? The sense of touch in our body is very important, and I am going to use it to illustrate a spiritual lesson. Touch gives us direct contact with our environment. Babies, animals, and all humans will die without touch. Animals have an instinct to lick their young. Babies must be held in order to thrive. Sensory nerve fibers are contained in your skin, which is the largest organ in your body. It weighs approximately six pounds and measures about two square yards—larger in some people.

There are one thousand to nine thousand sensory nerves per square inch of skin depending on the location in the body for obvious reasons: less on your back; more concentrated on your fingertips, lips, and the genital region, and the bottoms of the feet. These nerve endings enable us to feel things such as pleasurable touch, tickle, massage, holding hands, and kissing. However, they also allow us to feel pain, which warns us if something is too hot or sharp, so we quickly pull away to protect ourselves. The nerve endings rapidly carry the impulses to the brain so that we may react appropriately.

Humans have a strong desire to touch. Children always want to touch things, and parents spend a lot of time trying to teach them, "Don't touch." Adults have the same desire. What happens if you see a sign that says, "Wet paint—don't touch"? Eve, in the Garden of Eden, apparently had a desire to touch the forbidden fruit and yielded to the temptation of Satan.

You must have skin in order to have the sense of touch. God was untouchable before Christ came into the world. Jesus took upon Himself a body of flesh in order to have skin so that we could touch Him, and so He could feel our touch and feel our pain. Hebrews 4:15 tells us that He is touched with the feeling of our infirmities. This is possible because His earthly body had pain receptors in the skin, just like us, which enabled Him to feel our pain. He physically experienced the greatest intensity of pain known to man when He was crucified. In fact, we measure all other pain in comparison to the pain of crucifixion. We call severe pain "excruciating," which literally means "out of the cross or crucifixion." If you are experiencing pain at this moment, physically, spiritually, or emotionally, you can be assured, according to the Scripture, that Jesus has also experienced it as much or more, and that He understands and cares.

Under the Law, when Moses went up to Mount Sinai, no man or beast was allowed to touch the mountain or it would die (Heb. 12:20). The Law says, "Touch not, taste not, handle not." Grace says, "Reach out and touch the Lord."

The tabernacle in the wilderness was covered by skins of animals, and it was God's dwelling place on the earth. It represented Christ, who became a man, flesh, covered with skin. John 1:14 states, "And the Word was made flesh, and dwelt [tabernacled] among us." That Word was Jesus, Himself, born of a virgin. He was God veiled in a body of flesh so He could walk among men and bring God's presence to us. He was Emmanuel—God with us.

In John 20:25–28, we read the story of how "Doubting Thomas" insisted that he must touch Jesus' scars before he would believe that He was risen from the dead. When Jesus appeared to him, He invited him to do just that. Jesus is still inviting us to reach out and touch Him today. He says, "Come unto me, all ye that labor and are heavy laden, and I will give you rest" (Matt. 11:28).

Dr. Luke, the physician who wrote the gospel of Luke, relates the stories of two women in particular who reached out and touched Jesus, indicating that he, as a doctor, understood the importance of touch. Both women were unclean according to the Law, but they were unclean only until they touched Jesus. Luke 7:36–39 tells the story of a woman, "a sinner," who went into the Pharisee's house where Jesus was. She began weeping and washing Jesus' feet with her tears, then wiped them with her hair, kissed His feet, and anointed them with ointment. The Pharisee was repulsed by the fact that Jesus was allowing her to touch Him. But Jesus received pleasure from this act of love and kindness, because He knew her heart. He told her in verse 48, "...Thy sins are forgiven," and "...Thy faith hath saved thee..." in verse 50. No specific sin was mentioned in order that this woman could represent all repentant sinners who come to the feet of Jesus, "for all have sinned, and come short of the glory of God" (Rom. 3:23).

In the second story, Luke 8:43–46, Luke relates the incident of a woman which had an issue of blood for twelve years and had spent all of her money on physicians and could not be healed. This woman, according to the Mosaic Law, was also unclean due to her bloody discharge. Desperately she crawled through the crowd struggling to get close enough to Jesus to touch Him. As soon as she touched the border of His garment, she was healed, and Jesus said, "Who touched Me?" Many people were thronging Jesus, pushing and shoving Him, but only one person touched Him in faith and received from Him. Not a word was spoken, just a gentle contact and a life was changed. What about our lives? Do we really touch Jesus, or do we just go to church and "bump" into Him? If we touch Him in faith, our lives will be changed, and we are cleansed. Then we can reach out and touch others through the life of Christ in us.

Lastly, Jesus is not only touched by our infirmities and our needs, but He is also touched by our love and wants us to embrace Him. In the Song of Songs, we see a picture of Christ wooing us to be His bride. His desire is that we would love Him above all else, desiring to lean upon His breast, as did John the beloved disciple. One example of this kind of love is in Song of Songs 2:6: "His left hand is under my head, and his right hand doth embrace me." He wants us to return that embrace, as in Song of Songs 3:4: "...I found him whom my soul loveth: I held him, and would not let him go...." In Song of Songs 5:16, the Shulamite exclaims, "His mouth is most sweet: yea, he is altogether lovely." She knew him intimately and desired his loving gentle touch.

Also, we read in Song of Songs 1:2: "Let him kiss me with the kisses of his mouth...." Kissing is a pleasurable, touching expression of love. He kisses us with the Word of

His mouth as we read it and allow the Holy Spirit to touch our hearts. We kiss Him back with our praise and our love and submission to His will in our lives.

In Philippians 3:12–14, Paul's desire was to lay hold of (apprehend or embrace) Christ and be apprehended of Him, just like the Shulamite woman in the Song of Songs. Reach out and touch Him in faith and love, embrace Him and the Word of God, and your life will be changed forever.

SPIRITUAL HEARING
AND BALANCE

"So then faith cometh by hearing, and hearing by the word of God" (Rom. 10:17). What does it mean to *hear* the Word of God? The Word of God is of no value unless you really and truly *hear* it.

The physical act of hearing involves more than just channeling sound through the outer pieces of skin on the sides of your head that hold your glasses in place. I am going to explain the process of hearing in the physical so that you can better understand it in the spiritual. I will try not to get too technical, but I want you to catch a glimpse of the wonder of creation in the body.

The prophet Amos speaks about a famine of hearing the Word of God. It seems as though other nations are more eager to hear and heed the Word of God than is the United States. There are many voices in this world, and we have a choice regarding what we wish to listen to and what we tune our ears to hear.

Amos 8:11 states: "Behold, the days come, saith the LORD God, that I will send a famine in the land, not a famine of bread, nor a thirst for water, but of *hearing* the words of the LORD." I believe that time is here. God does not say there will be a famine of the Word of the Lord, but a famine of *hearing* the Word.

In Luke 9:44 Jesus said, "Let these sayings sink down into your ears." Physically there must be nothing in the ears that blocks the transmission of sound, so I am going to discuss various things that might do that.

Hearing the Word begins with an external sound, but it must reach all the way down to the inside, to the heart. Why is the Word of God so important? Not only because faith comes by hearing, but because life and hearing also come from the Word of God.

In Ezekiel 37:4, God told Ezekiel to prophesy to the dry bones in the valley and say unto them, "O ye dry bones, hear the word of the LORD." *Hear!* When you really *hear* the Word of God, it brings life. It is living and powerful and brought life to those dry bones. It must penetrate all the way from the outer ear to the spiritual inner ear and enlighten the heart.

The physical structure of hearing is composed of three parts (a trinity): the outer ear, the middle ear, and the inner ear. As we go through this, you will see there is more than one trinity (in fact there are three) in the ear.

The outer ear consists of a piece of flesh, called the auricle, which acts like a funnel, on both sides of your head, designed to pick up the sound in front of you and direct it inward to a hole leading to a channel called the auditory canal. From there the sound travels inward to the eardrum (the tympanic membrane), causing it to vibrate, then through the middle ear bones and on to the inner ear, which contains the organ of hearing. I will explain that in further detail as we go through it, along with the spiritual meaning. The outer ear can be likened to the Holy Spirit, who takes the Word of God and brings it to us. The Holy Spirit draws us to Christ, who is the middle man (the middle ear) between us and God (the inner ear).

The function of the outer ear is to catch the sound and to channel it inward to the eardrum. We can tune our ear to the things we want to hear by turning our head in the direction of the sound or turn it away from what we do not want to hear. We can cover up our ears so that we cannot hear it or amplify the sound to hear it better.

In the natural, doctors warn you not to put anything in your ears smaller than your elbow. Sometimes people try to clean their ears with cotton swabs, which only push the wax against the drum and pack it in, thus creating a plug that decreases hearing. In addition, people use objects such as keys, bobby pins, or the eraser end of a pencil to scratch their itching ears. This can create irritation and swelling, resulting in pain and decreased hearing. I have found some interesting things in ears when patients come in to the office complaining that they can't hear and want their ears checked (yes, even a pencil eraser)!

Spiritually our hearing is affected in the outer ear when we resist the Holy Spirit. Things from the world can come between us and hearing the Word of God, preventing us from hearing His still, small voice. We often come up with excuses as to why we can't make it to church or Bible study or we don't have the time to read the Word and allow it to speak to us.

We find an example of this in Acts 7:54–60, which relates the story of the stoning of Stephen. Verse 54 tells us, "When they heard these things, they were cut to the heart...." They heard the Word of God with the outer ear, but they did not like what they heard, because it brought conviction. That is the function of the Holy Spirit—to convince and convict of sin. Then we have a choice to make, either to hear and heed the Word or to turn away from it. We can choose to repent or to resist.

What did they do? Verse 57 tells us: "Then they cried with a loud voice, and stopped their ears...." They put their hands over their ears, or perhaps they put their fingers in their ears, because they did not want to hear any more of the Word that had pierced their hearts. They also cried out with a loud voice and made noise to drown out Stephen's sermon that was convicting them of sin.

Isaiah 42:23 asks a question: "Who among you will give ear to this? who will hearken and hear for the time to come?" The act of listening was described in this question: give ear (turn your head toward the sound, do not turn away) and hearken (pay attention and heed).

Have you ever watched a dog when it hears a sound? The ears will be hanging down when all of a sudden, the ears stand straight up to try to catch the sound, and it looks around. It is hearkening to it, paying attention and heeding it by perking up its ears. That is what we should do spiritually when we hear the Word of God; not just for now, but for the time to come.

We have a choice regarding what we wish to hear and how much of it. What is the world listening to today? Second Timothy 4:3–4 gives us the answer. Verse 3 states: "For the time will come when they will not endure sound doctrine;

but after their own lusts [desires] shall they heap to themselves teachers, having itching ears." Itching occurs in the outer ear. These are ears that listen to only what they *want* to hear, what they are "itching" to hear.

Verse 4 states: "And they shall turn away their ears from the truth...." That is a purposeful turning away after they hear the truth. You cannot turn away from something you have not heard. If you hear a sound but you don't like it, you can choose to turn away from it. They refused to hear the truth. Do not feel sorry for them; pray for them, but don't feel sorry. They have heard and turned away. It takes an effort to turn away. Verse 4 continues: "...and shall be turned unto fables." If they are not heeding the Word, what are they heeding? Anything else is not the truth; it is a fable, a fairy tale, a lie. They stop up their ears from hearing the truth and turn unto "cunningly devised fables" (2 Peter 1:16).

But we have "a more sure word of prophecy; whereunto ye do well that ye take heed" (2 Peter 1:19). We must hear, hearken, and heed. The outer ear gives us a picture of the ministry of the Holy Spirit, which is to draw us to Christ and reveal His Word. You can heed the wooing of the Holy Spirit, or you can purposely turn away.

Now let us proceed to the middle ear situated between the outer ear and the inner ear. It spiritually represents Christ, who is the "middle man," or the Mediator between us and God. The Holy Spirit brings us to Christ, who brings us to God.

The outer ear ends at the eardrum. Between the eardrum and the inner ear lies the middle ear, which is a space filled with air containing three bones or ossicles (another trinity).

A tube, called the eustachian tube, equalizes the air pressure and allows drainage to keep the space from filling up with fluid or infection, which could hinder the movement of or destroy the ossicles, resulting in hearing loss.

The three bones (ossicles) are called the malleus, incus, and stapes, and they are connected to each other in succession. These are more commonly known as the hammer, the anvil, and the stirrup due to their shapes. The sound waves are channeled from the outer ear to the eardrum, which then vibrates at that frequency. The eardrum is attached to the first ossicle, the malleus. The ossicles are arranged in such a manner as to amplify the sound as the vibrations are transmitted along them. The vibration of the eardrum converts the sound waves from the air into mechanical energy, which is carried along the ossicles as they vibrate.

The third ossicle, the stapes, has a tiny oval foot pedal on it that inserts into a small window, called the oval window, the first part of the inner ear. Its action is similar to that of a piston in a car. The inner ear is filled with fluid and the foot pedal of the stapes is pushed into that fluid, resulting in movement of the fluid. This in turn vibrates the hair cells in the cochlea (the organ of hearing), which I will discuss shortly.

The middle ear is dependent on the movement of the eardrum. Likewise, the Holy Spirit must move upon us to enable us to understand the Word of God. Without the Holy Spirit we can read the Word, but it has little meaning. Anything that obstructs the movement of the eardrum and the middle ear bones impairs the hearing, which has a spiritual comparison.

In Acts 7:51 we read part of Stephen's sermon in which he calls the Christ rejectors "ye stiffnecked and uncircumcised in heart and ears, ye do always resist the Holy Ghost." The act of circumcision in the natural involves cutting away, in a circle, the excess skin called the foreskin. But what about circumcision of the ears?

After repeated middle ear infections, scar tissue can build up against the eardrum and hinder its movement. This is dead tissue or "proud flesh." Spiritually speaking, the flesh gets in the way of hearing the Word of God and must be cut away. A doctor removes this surgically by cutting around the eardrum (similar to circumcision) and pulls it back to clean out all of the dead flesh and scar tissue that affects the movement of the eardrum and the ossicles. We must allow the Great Physician to circumcise our spiritual eardrum from fleshly things that cause us to resist the movement of the Holy Ghost. It is the cutting away of the flesh, which enables us to continue to *hear* the Word of God.

From here we can progress to the inner ear, which represents God Himself. It is quite amazing and complex, but I will try to simplify it. The inner ear is composed of two parts, the organ of hearing (the cochlea) and the organ of balance (the labyrinth). It seems strange that these two seemingly separate systems are located together in the inner ear, but as you will see this has an important meaning spiritually.

The cochlea has the appearance of a small snail. This is where the innermost ossicle of the middle ear, the stapes, fits into the oval window, like a piston, forcing the fluid to vibrate. The fluid inside the cochlea then vibrates at the same frequency of the sound waves on the outside. In the cochlea there are 24,000 hair cells (nerve fibers), which are arranged in groups based on the frequency at which they vibrate. In other words, if you hit a certain note on the piano, those specific hair cells will vibrate. So, you can have hearing loss at one frequency but not at another. If you are exposed to too loud a noise at a certain frequency, it will force the fluid vibrating those hair cells so hard that it will destroy them. It shears them off, much like trees in a hurricane.

Because sound can become a very powerful force by the time it reaches the inner ear, God designed the middle ear to actually have tiny muscles alongside the eardrum, next to the ossicles, that can dampen the sound. If you are exposed to excessive noise, the muscles will tighten to limit the vibrations and help protect the inner ear from damage. Spiritually this means that the Holy Spirit and Christ can enable us to resist the things of the world and Satan. We can tune them out by God's power. However, if we continually put ourselves in the wrong environment, we are going to end up having some hearing damage, both physically and spiritually.

For every sound there are hair cells that will vibrate at that specific frequency, and those vibrations are converted into chemical energy, which is transmitted along the auditory nerve to the brain enabling you to hear it. Not only do you hear a sound, but you understand what it was that was said or you recognize what it was. You think, "Oh, that is the sound of a bird," or you recognize someone's voice.

In John 10, Jesus tells us that His sheep *hear* His voice and *know* His voice, meaning they know *who* He is and *what* He is saying. Sometimes people speak in a manner that is difficult to understand, but if you are around them enough, you learn their voice and can understand them. The more we read or hear the Word of God, the more we recognize the Shepherd's voice and what He is saying to us.

Matthew 13 records the parable of the sower. You may not think of this parable as being a parable about hearing, but it is. Jesus says to them in verse 9: "Who hath ears to hear, let him hear." He is again admonishing them to let His sayings sink down into their ears. This is not just a story about a farmer who went to plant seeds or how we ought to plow our ground. There is far more to it than that.

In verse 10, the disciples asked Jesus, "Why speakest thou unto them in parables? He answered and said unto them, Because it is given unto *you* to know the mysteries of the kingdom of heaven, but to them it is not given." They did not know His voice! Verse 13 continues, "Therefore speak I to them in parables: because they seeing see not; and hearing they hear not, neither do they understand."

Verse 15 states, "For this people's heart is waxed gross [grown heavy], and their ears are dull of hearing." What does this mean? It means they cannot hear with their hearts. Dull of hearing is "hard of listening." You can be hard of hearing and truly not hear, or you can be "hard of listening" and just not *want* to hear. Verse 15 finishes with "…and their eyes have they closed; lest at any time they should see with their eyes, and hear with their ears, and should understand with their heart…." If they hear with their ears and the saying sinks all the way down into their heart, then they will understand.

Verse 18 states: "Hear ye therefore the parable of the sower." Listen to what it means! He knew that His disciples had no idea what it meant, either, so He explained it to them.

Verse 20 states: "But he that received the seed into stony places, the same is he that heareth the word, and anon with joy receiveth it." But it has no root; it doesn't get past the outer ear. You may say, "That was a beautiful sermon." But does it have any meaning to you? Did it touch your heart? When you really *hear* it with your ears, it touches the heart and bears fruit.

Verse 22 states: "He also that received seed among the thorns is he that heareth the word; and the care of this world, and the deceitfulness of riches, choke the word and he becometh unfruitful." It is like having scar tissue, uncircumcised ears, which keep the eardrum and ossicles from vibrating; thus, the word never gets past the middle ear, and there is no understanding.

Verse 23 states: "But he that received seed into the good ground is he that heareth the word, and understandeth it; which also beareth fruit." The only way you can understand it is when it reaches all the way to the inner ear, to the cochlea, stimulating the hair cells and traveling along the auditory nerve to the brain. Each individual has the choice to decide if they want to hear and heed the Word of God or turn away from it, stopping their ears. We must let it sink all the way down into our hearts and *hear* what God is saying to us.

What about the second part of the inner ear, the labyrinth, which is the balance center? Why are the organs of hearing and balance combined in the inner ear? The cochlea is filled with fluid and is floating in fluid, and so is the labyrinth. When you move your head, they are both supported by the fluid, as is a baby in the womb, and not tossed around and damaged.

The labyrinth is composed of three loops called semicircular canals (another trinity). They are connected at ninety-degree angles like the corner of a room and function similarly to a level, so that your brain knows what position your body is in at all times. No matter which way you turn your body, your brain can navigate you to keep you from falling. There must be an engineer involved somewhere in this!

I think it is amazing that the organs of hearing and balance are associated with each other in the physical body since it is so true in the spiritual. God created the body so that hearing and standing are related. Isn't that incredible? You would think that they were two separate functions, but God combined them in the inner ear. I think it is because in the spiritual we stand by hearing. It is the Word of God, once we *hear* it, that is able to keep us from falling.

In order to stand spiritually, we must know our position in Christ. How are we going to know that? By hearing the Word of God! When we read it, we need to *hear* His voice speaking to our hearts and believe it. Then by faith (which comes by hearing), we are able to stand.

Now for one more interesting fact about the inner ear: It is located inside the petrous bone in your skull. *Petrous* means "rock," and it is the hardest bone in your body. Therefore, the fragile organs of hearing and balance are both protected in the "cleft of the rock." This is where we are spiritually when we truly *hear* and stand on the Word of God, safely dwelling in the cleft of the Rock.

SPIRITUAL FOREIGN BODY
IN THE EYE

Have you ever had something get in your eye that you couldn't get out? A foreign body such as an eyelash is quite common. What usually happens is that the eye will start burning and watering, and your tears will wash it out. But that is not always the case, especially with other foreign bodies, such as a piece of metal or a speck of something the wind blew in.

If the foreign body stays in your eye, it soon becomes very painful, causing your eyelid to start spasming, and you will be unable to keep the eye open, making it difficult to see. This is called "blepharospasm," over which you have no control. The eye will also turn red from the irritation, and it has the potential to become infected if the foreign body is not removed. If it is not properly treated, it may cause permanent scarring to the cornea, resulting in visual loss.

The Bible refers to foreign bodies in the eye in Matthew 7:3–5, which, of course, has a spiritual meaning: "And why beholdest thou the mote [splinter or speck] that is in thy brother's eye, but considerest not the beam [plank] that is in thine own eye? Or how wilt thou say to thy brother, Let me pull out the mote out of thine eye; and, behold, a beam is in thine own eye? Thou hypocrite, first cast out the beam out of thine own eye; and, then shalt thou see clearly to cast out the mote out of thy brother's eye."

In the physical, a foreign body in the eye affects the ability to see clearly. The man in the parable was afflicted with a large foreign body that he was ignoring; and even though he would not be able to see it well, he was criticizing his brother for not taking care of a small problem (a speck in the eye) that he thought needed to be removed.

Hebrews 12:2 says we are to be "looking unto Jesus the author and finisher of our faith..." in order to run the race that is set before us. A spiritual foreign body is anything in our lives that takes our eyes off the Lord and puts them onto others or ourselves, or blocks the visual field between Him and us.

When we take our eyes off of Jesus, our goal, we begin to look at the other runners in the race to compare ourselves to them. If we can find even a small fault in them, then we can more easily excuse or overlook our own faults. However, in order to win the prize, we must get our eyes back on the goal. A runner must be willing to lay aside and remove everything that might slow him down or distract him in the race. Likewise, all spiritual foreign bodies must be removed from our eyes in order for us to be able to keep looking unto Jesus.

Now I am going to discuss foreign bodies in the natural and their treatment so that you may better understand spiritual foreign bodies and how they affect your daily Christian walk. A foreign body needs to be removed from the eye, for it is dangerous to leave in. It cannot be ignored; you must seek medical attention if you are unable to remove it.

The first treatment would be to wash the eye with pure water. Most of the time God uses tears, both physically and spiritually, to accomplish this. The pure water also represents the Word of God, as is seen in Ephesians 5:26: "That he might sanctify and cleanse it [the church] with the washing of water by the word."

We get dirt in our eyes every day, and our tears wash it out. Sometimes God allows painful circumstances in our lives, along with tears, to cleanse us from the dirt and contamination of this world and things that take our eyes off of Him. We also need a daily cleansing from His Word in order that we may see Jesus more clearly. It then allows us to see our brother's condition more clearly in order that we may pray for him and minister to his needs. In fact, that speck that we thought we saw might actually have been something in our own eyes.

A foreign body that enters the eye comes from two possible sources: 1) something from yourself (i.e., an eyelash), or 2) something from the world (dirt or debris). These have different meanings spiritually. Examples of that which comes from ourselves would be self-righteousness, pride in our own good works or position, selfishness, jealousy, anger, hatred, or covetousness, not to mention the lusts of the flesh.

That which comes from the world would be represented by man's religious ideas and programs, legality, or any teaching that lifts up a name other than Jesus. The daily cares and concerns of this life could also detract us from looking unto Jesus by keeping our eyes focused on our own affairs instead of Him.

What about the treatment? In order for a physician to remove the foreign body, a person must be in full submission and lie flat on the exam table, perfectly still, looking straight up. Numbing eye drops are then instilled. Immediately the person feels better and may think the problem is resolved since the pain is temporarily gone. However, the procedure has just begun. If the foreign body has been there for a while and is embedded in the cornea, the physician may need to take a needle with a sharp edge and gently scrape it away a little at a time, while wearing magnifying lenses. Once this is accomplished, the eye is again cleansed with eye wash.

Spiritually this means we need to be willing to rest in the Lord and let Him do the work. Sometimes we don't like to be still and allow God to work in our lives; we just don't have time for that. God said in 2 Chronicles 20:17: "Ye shall not need to fight in this battle: set yourselves, stand ye still, and see the salvation of the Lord with you...."

We need to let Him use the scalpel of the Word to skillfully remove the things in our lives that hinder us from keeping our eyes focused on Jesus. He knows exactly how deep to cut without causing us harm. Slowly, little by little, line upon line, precept upon precept, the Word of God whittles away at our spiritual foreign bodies, and then we are able to see Jesus more clearly. During this whole time, we must keep looking up and remain still, keeping our hands out of the way, resting in Him, trusting Him completely to do the work in us.

Following the removal of the foreign body, the physician may apply a healing antibiotic ointment to protect the cornea from infection while it heals. Spiritually this represents the anointing of the Holy Spirit, who comforts us and reveals to us God's purpose in our lives through His Word.

In Luke 7:37–48, we read the story of a woman who "was a sinner" who came to the Pharisee's house where Jesus had been invited to eat. She fell at Jesus' feet in repentance and began washing His feet with her tears and then anointed them with precious ointment after drying them with her hair. She had washed the foreign body out of her eyes and saw clearly who Jesus was, and He forgave her sins. The Pharisee, on the other hand, was spiritually blind because of the large plank in his eye. He was unable to see but had no desire to have his vision restored. Instead, he could only see the sinful condition of the woman compared to his own self-righteousness.

God addressed this pharisaical attitude when He spoke to the Laodicean church in Revelation 3:17–18 and said, "Because thou sayest, I am rich, and increased with goods, and have need of nothing; and knowest not that thou art wretched, and miserable, and poor, and blind, and naked: I counsel thee to buy of me gold tried in the fire, that thou mayest be rich; and white raiment, that thou mayest be clothed, and that the shame of thy nakedness do not appear; and anoint thine eyes with eyesalve, that thou mayest see."

It takes the anointing of the Holy Spirit, the eye salve, to open our eyes through the Word of God in order that we may see Jesus. Until then we are blind to our own sin and self-righteousness, as was the Pharisee in Jesus' day.

As Christians, we also need our eyes to be cleansed daily with the washing of the water of the Word in order to see clearly the goal that is set before us, so that we may run for the prize and win Christ as our Bridegroom.

INSTRUMENTS OF RIGHTEOUSNESS

Let not sin therefore reign in your mortal body, that ye should obey it in the lusts thereof. Neither yield ye your members as instruments of unrighteousness unto sin: but yield yourselves unto God, as those that are alive from the dead, and our members as instruments of unrighteousness unto sin: but yield yourselves unto God, as those that are alive from the dead, and your members as instruments of righteousness unto God.

—Romans 6:12–13

What is an instrument? It is a tool that is prepared for a specific purpose, such as a musical or surgical instrument. Since I am a physician, I am going to use the analogy of surgical instruments compared to us as members of the body of Christ and instruments of God. God performed the first surgery when He removed a rib from Adam to prepare a bride for him. He continues to perform surgery on the body, the church, and is in need of instruments. Even the simplest of surgeries requires a variety of instruments. God desires to use each one of us in a special way for a specific purpose. He has chosen us and purchased us with the blood of His Son.

No matter how good a surgeon is, he cannot perform surgery without instruments. The instruments do not possess any skill; the surgeon does. For each surgery, a group of instruments is necessary, not just one; and none of these are more important than the other. The value of each instrument is not based on its size, the brand name, or the previous surgeries for which it has been used, but on its intended use. Each one is of equal value when it is in the hands of the surgeon. Each instrument has been created for a specific purpose and will be used as the need arises. Some will be used more often than others, but each one must be clean and sterilized and prepared ahead of time in order to be used. God has fashioned each member of the body of Christ according to His plan and arranged us in a specific manner in much the same way as instruments on a surgical tray are laid out prior to surgery in preparation to be used when the surgeon calls for them. Just like the surgical instruments, each one of us is unique and valuable to the Lord, but we must be willing to work together and wait on the Lord for His timing. We must also yield to the necessary cleansing process that prepares us for service, for the ministry He has chosen for us.

Each surgical instrument must be cleansed initially and after each surgery or anytime it becomes contaminated. Instruments in a hospital are taken to Central Supply for a thorough scrubbing and cleansing wash. In 2 Corinthians 7:1, Paul instructs that we are to "cleanse ourselves from all filthiness of the flesh and spirit, perfecting holiness in the fear of God." An instrument cannot cleanse itself; it simply has to yield to the cleansing process that has been provided. We are to *let* Him cleanse us through His Word, as is stated in Ephesians 5:26: "That he might sanctify and cleanse it [the church] with the washing of water by the word." What does it mean to sanctify something? It means to set it apart or separate it for a specific purpose. Not only does He cleanse us, but He must separate us from the world in order to be useful as His instruments.

After surgical instruments are cleansed, they must be sterilized. Prior to sterilization, an instrument is placed in a special package that is capable of withstanding heat, and it is sealed so that the instrument is completely separated from anything that could contaminate it. Then it is put into a sterilizer, which is heated to a specific temperature to kill any residual bacteria. It remains in that package with a seal on it, signifying that it is ready to be used when the surgeon needs it.

Sterilized instruments are not *better* instruments. They are the same instruments, but they are better *prepared*, for they have not only been cleansed but separated and sealed. As God's instruments we also must be cleansed, separated, sealed, and put "through the fire" in order to be declared instruments of righteousness. We are to be separated from the world, for we are *in* the world but not *of* the world. God instructs us to do this in 2 Corinthians 6:17: "Come out from among them, and be ye separate, saith the Lord, and touch not the unclean thing." It is only then that we can be deemed suitable for service. We don't like the scrubbing or the separation, and we certainly don't enjoy the fiery trials, but it is only through this process that He can purify us.

It is the Holy Spirit that separates us unto God. Paul was considered by God to be a "chosen vessel," but he had to be separated for service, as we read in Acts 13:2: "The Holy Ghost said, Separate me Barnabas and Saul [Paul] for the work whereunto I have called them." What about the seal? Ephesians 1:13 answers that question: "After that ye believed, ye were sealed with that holy Spirit of promise." So, you see that the Holy Spirit not only separates us, but He seals us for service. Our job is to yield to the Holy Spirit and let Him do the work in us.

If a sterilized instrument falls during surgery and becomes contaminated, it is not thrown away, for it is too valuable to be discarded. It is picked up, cleansed, and put "through the fire" again so that it may be used at another time. Likewise, there are times when we may stumble and fall but God does not discard us. We are too valuable to Him, for He paid a great price for us. First, He picks us up. This is described in Psalm 37:23–24: "The steps of a good man are ordered by the LORD.... Though he fall, he shall not be utterly cast down: for the LORD upholdeth him with his hand." Then comes the cleansing so that He may use us: "If we confess our sins, he is faithful and just to forgive us our sins, and to cleanse us from all unrighteousness" (1 John 1:9). We are also exposed daily to the contamination of this world and need a daily cleansing from the water of the Word of God.

During the time that a fallen contaminated instrument is being re-sterilized, the surgeon has to substitute with a different sterile instrument in order to finish the surgery. We must remain yielded and separated at all times, for God may need to use us outside of our "calling." Remember, it is the skill of the surgeon that is important, not ours. Our job is simply to yield our physical members as instruments of righteousness in His hands.

Many different types of instruments are needed during a surgery to perform the multitude of required tasks. Some are very small and may seem insignificant, while others are quite large, but all are necessary. This is also true in the body of

Christ. For example, a scalpel is first needed to do the cutting. This would represent the Word of God, which is "sharper than any twoedged sword" (Heb. 4:12), that is given out by the ministers. Then retractors are used to pull back the tissues and hold things out of the way. These could represent prayer warriors who hold back the forces of the enemy (Satan) by their prayers. Without retractors it would be very difficult to perform surgery. Forceps are necessary to pick up things. Spiritually, we are instructed to "lift up" the hands that hang down, to comfort and help those in need. Various clamps are needed to hold things or bring things together, which is also an important ministry in the body of Christ. I could use other examples, but I think you get the idea by now that we each have a ministry that God has given us to perform, and that we are valuable to Him. God did not choose us because we were valuable. We are valuable because He chose us.

God is capable of taking anyone, no matter how defiled and dirty they may be, and transforming them into an instrument of righteousness. I would like to illustrate this by relating an experience I had while on a medical mission trip to a third world country a number of years ago. On that particular trip, a group of plumbers and other handymen had also come for the purpose of trying to restore water and repair plumbing, including toilets, in the hospital where the surgical team was to be working. A patient was brought to the hospital who needed a surgery that required orthopedic instruments, but none were available. One of the doctors realized that the plumbers' tools were similar to what was needed and suggested that perhaps they could be cleaned and sterilized and used for the surgery. So that is exactly what happened. The filthy tools that had been used the day before to fix toilets were scrubbed and sterilized and became servants of the surgeon instead of the plumber. They had been transformed from dirty to clean, and the surgery was able to be performed successfully.

This is also what God can do for us. He sees our potential to become His instruments, and by the blood of Jesus, He is able to transform us from servants of sin into instruments of righteousness. All we need to do is to be willing to yield ourselves to Him and be cleansed.

SPIRITUAL BREASTFEEDING

"And when Abram was ninety years old and nine, the LORD appeared to Abram, and said unto him, I am the Almighty God; walk before me, and be thou perfect" (Gen. 17:1). God revealed Himself to Abraham as the "Almighty God," which is actually *El Shaddai* in the Hebrew. *El* or *Elohim* means "God" and signifies the "strong one" or the "all-sufficient one." *Shaddai* is from the Hebrew word *shad*, used in Scripture for a woman's breast, as in Psalm 22:9: "But thou art he that took me out of the womb: thou didst make me hope when I was on my mother's breasts."

El Shaddai therefore signifies loving strength as the all-sufficient, never-failing breast that nourishes, strengthens, and satisfies.

First Peter 2:2 admonishes us, "As newborn babes, desire the sincere milk of the word, that ye may grow thereby." "Sincere" means "tested and found pure." Breast milk is sincere, pure, unadulterated (nothing added, nothing taken away), always fresh, warm, and readily available.

The best claim that a formula company can make is that theirs is nearest to mothers' milk. Doctors recommend breastfeeding whenever possible because of the many health and emotional benefits it can provide. This is true spiritually, as well. Bible study books and commentaries may be helpful, but they are no substitute for the pure Word of God.

Breast milk not only contains the proper amount of protein, calcium, and sugar for growth, but it also provides immune protection from the mother's body to fight off infection. The mother's own "power" to overcome illness is passed through the breast milk in the form of antibodies to her newborn, who has no protection of its own. This means that the "battle" for the baby's health was already fought by the mother before the baby was actually born. Likewise, the spiritual victory for our souls was won at Calvary before we had our spiritual new birth.

Breast milk is produced in more than sufficient quantities to satisfy the baby's hunger and need. The more a baby desires and suckles, the more milk is produced, as sucking triggers the mother's pituitary gland to release a hormone called prolactin, which increases the milk supply. In other words, the greater the demand, the greater the supply. A hungry baby will always have a more-than-sufficient supply of milk. John 6:35 assures us that we will be satisfied if we feed on the Word: "...he that cometh to me shall never hunger; and he that believeth on me shall never thirst."

Babies require physical contact with their mothers, not just milk, or they will not survive. Breast feeding supplies both, for it necessitates the mother's presence, closeness, and touch. The usual position for breastfeeding a newborn baby requires one of the mother's arms to be underneath and around the baby, fully supporting its body, while the other hand supports the head. Song of Songs 2:6 describes a similar position: "His left hand is under my head and his right hand doth embrace me." Likewise, in Deuteronomy 33:27, we read, "...underneath are the everlasting arms...."

The instruction of Peter to "desire the sincere milk" implies that we should not only hunger for His Word, but also for the closeness and presence of the Lord as He lovingly presses us to His breast to feed. We must recognize our utter and complete dependence on Him for our daily needs and rest securely in His everlasting arms, just as if we were newborn babes.

No matter how much we grow and mature in the Lord, we should never outgrow our desire for His loving embrace. John, called the Beloved Apostle, leaned on Jesus' breast, for he recognized that in addition to nourishment, the breast is a place of comfort, safety, and love, close to the heart. In fact, in the natural, a crying baby can be comforted by listening to its mother's heartbeat.

A woman has two breasts, and her baby should suck at both breasts, alternating from side to side. Not only does this equalize the milk supply, but it allows balanced development of eye-hand coordination, since the baby uses opposite eye and hand movements while sucking at each breast.

Spiritually, God desires us to study both the Old and New Testaments (to suck at both breasts) in order to gain a better understanding of His divine purposes. All Scripture is given by inspiration of God and is profitable. The hidden treasures of the Old Testament are revealed to us by the Holy Spirit in the New Testament.

In Isaiah 49:15, God asks the question, "Can a mother forget her sucking child?" Yes, but not for long, for she soon has a physical reminder. A breastfeeding mother has a unique relationship with her baby. When her baby cries, she experiences a tingling sensation in her breasts called the "let-down reflex." The brain signals the release of a hormone called oxytocin that causes the milk to start flowing, even before the baby begins to suck!

If a mother does not breastfeed for too long of a period of time, the breasts will become engorged and painful from an oversupply. She then welcomes the cry and suckling of her baby, for it brings relief as the milk begins to flow. Likewise, our heavenly Father, *El Shaddai*, is tuned to the cries of His children and is ready and eagerly waiting to answer. He knows what we have need of even before we ask. It hurts Him if we do not call upon His name when we are in need. The "effectual, fervent prayer of a righteous man" will trigger that "let-down reflex" of *El Shaddai*, and He will supply exceedingly, abundantly above all that we ask or think.

The Word of God is "quick [living] and powerful," full of antibodies, as long as it is sincere, not watered down, pasteurized, or fortified by man's ideas. The power of the blood is passed into the milk of the Word and is readily available to those who "hunger and thirst after righteousness" and unashamedly (as a newborn babe) suckle at the breasts of *El Shaddai*.

SPIRITUAL OSTEOPOROSIS

What is osteoporosis? I am going to answer that question by first discussing the physical condition and its consequences and then applying that to the spiritual body with examples from Scripture. *Osteoporosis* is a word composed of two parts: *osteo* meaning "bone" and *porosis* meaning "porous or full of holes." Osteoporosis occurs when the body's bony skeleton loses calcium, stored as bone, faster than it can be replaced, and it is most common in the spine, hips, and wrists. As a result, the bones become weak and fragile and are easily fractured, even from a minor trauma such as coughing, bending over, or a low-impact fall from a standing height. If osteoporosis is severe enough, one can even fracture a hip from bearing the weight of their own body when walking.

With time, if the osteoporosis is not treated, a person may begin developing a curvature in the upper back called a "Dowager's Hump," as the spine actually collapses from the mere pull of gravity. Eventually the person is no longer able to walk upright. This has a spiritual meaning, which I will discuss shortly.

If you are older than the age of fifty, you have a 50 percent chance of a fracture in your lifetime. Bone loss begins around age thirty and declines most rapidly in women after menopause or a hysterectomy. Approximately eight million women have osteoporosis, and 2.2 million are at risk. Men also can develop osteoporosis, but it is not as common until they are older. The annual cost burden for osteoporosis and subsequent fractures is greater than fourteen billion dollars in the United States alone.

The Bible records a textbook picture of osteoporosis in Luke 13:11–13: "And behold, there was a woman which had a spirit of infirmity eighteen years, and was bowed together, and could in no wise lift up herself. And when Jesus saw her, he called her to him, and said unto her, Woman, thou art loosed from thine infirmity. And he laid his hands on her: and immediately she was made straight, and glorified God." The woman in the story obviously had severe osteoporosis with multiple compression fractures of the spine and had to walk bent over with a cane as she was unable to walk upright. But Jesus spoke the word and she was able to stand up straight.

Spiritual osteoporosis is evident when a person is unable to walk uprightly or stand against the wiles of the devil (Eph. 6:11). But there is no reason to despair, as there is healing available for us, just as it was for that woman through the Word if we hear it and obey it and yield to the touch of the hand of the Lord. Likewise, there are treatments and preventive measures for physical osteoporosis. But in order to better understand the causes and treatments, let us first examine the process by which bone is formed in the human body.

Ecclesiastes 11:5 states, "...the bones do grow in the womb of her that is with child." This is a medically accurate statement, as the gestational age of a baby in utero is determined by a sonogram that measures bone length. The length of the femur (thigh bone) gives a close estimate of the baby's age. Bones start out as cartilage, which forms the skeleton. Then as the fetus grows, calcium, phosphorous, and magnesium in the proper proportions are deposited along this cartilaginous matrix. The deposition of minerals begins in the middle of the bones and proceeds toward the ends. At the ends of the bones are located the growth plates, which remain as cartilage until a child reaches full stature, and then they calcify. At this point growth ceases.

Bone is a living tissue that can repair itself easily, especially when we are young, if it has adequate building materials, such as vitamin D, calcium, and appropriate signals from the body to start the process. The regulation of this process is very complex and involves the interaction of hormones from the parathyroid and thyroid glands, as well as kidneys and various other hormones in the body that activate the bone cells. Bone has two types of cells, those that build up (osteoblasts) and those that tear down (osteoclasts), which are activated by these hormones, depending on the need.

Bone structure is not solid like cement. If it were, you would be too heavy to walk. It is similar to latticework with crisscrossing girders of bone that stabilize and support each other like the undergirding of a bridge. In like manner, bone requires regular maintenance to remain strong or it will collapse.

Bones increase in density until around age thirty, as the body deposits more calcium to make the girders thicker and stronger. When osteoporosis develops, these girders become thinner and weaker, and some of them collapse. The density, or strength, of a bone can be measured with a special type of X-ray called a Dexa Scan.

In the Bible, there are multiple references relating to diseased bones that are applicable to the soul as well as the body. In Psalm 6:2, David states, "...my bones are vexed." Proverbs 12:4 refers to "rottenness of bones."

What are some of the things in our lives that can affect us spiritually and tear us down, causing us to be unable to stand against Satan (i.e., spiritual rottenness of bones)? Pride, self-pity, self-consciousness, self-works—all of these take our eyes off of Jesus and put them onto the self.

Proverbs 16:18 declares that pride goes before a fall. If you have severe osteoporosis, your hip can break before you fall, just from standing or walking. Pride, like osteoporosis, can result in an unexpected fall. Pride in our own works or accomplishments lifts up self instead of Christ and weakens us spiritually. Our true standing before God is only in the work of Calvary wrought by Christ when He died for our sins.

First Cor. 10:12 warns us, "...let him that thinketh he standeth take heed lest he fall." We cannot stand in our own strength. We must *know* that we stand in His grace alone (Rom. 5:1–2) and His might (Eph. 6:10–11) and not just *think* that we stand.

Jesus had strong bones. He was in the prime of His life, His early thirties, the age at which bone density reaches its maximum. Satan was unable to break His bones or make Him fall. In Exodus 12:46, Israel was specifically commanded regarding the Passover lamb that none of its bones should be broken. Psalm 34:20 is a prophecy concerning Jesus stating, "He keepeth all his bones: not one of them is broken." This was fulfilled in John 19:33, 36, which states, "...they brake not his legs...that the scripture should be fulfilled, A bone of him shall not be broken." If we have the life of Christ in us, and we appropriate and lay hold of that truth, then we will also be able to stand against Satan without fear of falling, as in Ephesians 6:11. Therefore Satan has no power to break our spiritual legs, either.

Next, I would like to address the prevention of osteoporosis. What can be done to maintain good bone health? What are your risk factors, and what can be done to change some of them, both physically and spiritually?

Age and genetics are two risk factors over which we have no control, but if you have a family history of osteoporosis, you should be even more vigilant to correct the other risk factors that can be altered.

Smoking is a very strong risk factor, a habit that is harmful in many ways, but God is able to deliver you from this if you will let Him. There are also multiple medications available from your doctor that can assist you in quitting; however, you must first purpose in your heart that you *want* to quit, or you will not succeed. The bondage of smoking is like the bondage of sin. It has control of you, and until you recognize that you are enslaved, you will not seek to be set free.

Inadequate calcium intake is another risk factor. Your bones act as a storage bank for calcium, a mineral necessary for muscle relaxation as well as many other processes in the body. When your blood calcium level gets too low, the body releases special hormones to draw calcium from your "bone bank" by activating the osteoclasts. If this continues, you will become overdrawn at the bank, resulting in a deficit that we call osteoporosis. You must make a daily deposit of sufficient calcium (1,000 to 1,500 mg in two or three divided doses) to maintain your "bone bank" balance. Spiritually we need to "...desire the sincere milk of the word..." (1 Pet. 2:2), and partake of it in sufficient quantities daily.

Some churches today no longer preach the "sincere milk of the word" and have concocted a religious beverage that peps you up, tastes sweet, and makes you feel good rather than nourishing the soul. People are being fed a watered-down version of the true milk and never seem to develop a desire to drink of it between Sunday morning services. Likewise, in the American diet, milk is frequently being replaced by carbonated, sweetened, highly caffeinated beverages or excessively strong coffee. Soda pop is high in phosphorus and sodium. Excess phosphorus blocks the absorption of calcium, and high sodium and high caffeine intake cause a loss of calcium in the urine. Such beverages should be avoided spiritually and physically to prevent "...rottenness of bones," as in Proverbs 12:4.

First Timothy 4:7 instructs us to exercise ourselves unto godliness. A sedentary lifestyle or inadequate exercise can lead to osteoporosis as well as several other health problems. Walking is one of the easiest and safest types for people of all ages and costs nothing. First John 1:7 tells us to "...walk in the light, as he is in the light...". This is important physically also, as sunlight is a valuable source of vitamin D, which is necessary for calcium absorption. Ultraviolet rays from the sun cause a chemical reaction in the skin that produces vitamin D. This process requires unprotected sunlight exposure for fifteen minutes and should be repeated on a daily basis for maximum benefit.

Seventy percent of women age fifty to seventy lack vitamin D, and 90 percent of those over seventy are lacking. This is largely due to spending too much time inside under artificial lighting, therefore you should make sure your calcium supplement contains vitamin D. Recent studies have also shown that many children are at risk for vitamin D deficiency due to inadequate time playing outside. Because of technological advancements, the trend is to spend our leisure time inside playing video games or using the computer or other electronics, resulting in a lack of physical activity and sunshine exposure.

Weight-bearing exercise is essential to prevent osteoporosis. Bones require stress, such as the pull of gravity from walking in order to remain strong. Prolonged bedrest, more than two or three days, can quickly lead to bone loss. When the astronauts first journeyed to the moon and back, spending an extended period of time in weightlessness, it was discovered that they had lost significant bone mass. They were so weak upon their return that they required assistance to stand up against the force of gravity. Now astronauts are required to do resistance-type exercises while in space daily to prevent this.

Even though bones are strengthened by stress, and inactivity or lack of gravity will weaken them, we must be careful not to *over*stress the body, which could lead to stress fractures. Spiritually we must all endure a certain amount of trials in our Christian lives in order to gain strength. But God has promised that He would not put on us more than we are able to bear. However, sometimes we take upon ourselves too heavy a burden by failing to cast our cares upon Him and letting Him help carry our load. If you try to lift more than you are capable of carrying, physically or spiritually, it may result in a compression fracture of the spine. It is far better to seek assistance from someone who is stronger than you or to share the burden with another. Jesus promised that if we are yoked together with Him, the burden would be light (Matt. 4:28–30).

Another factor that can put you at risk for osteoporosis relates to the prolonged use of certain medications, including steroids, antiseizure, and thyroid drugs, which may speed up bone loss. Even certain types of birth control hormones can result in osteoporosis: If you are taking any of these, you should have a Dexa Scan (bone density test), and you may need to start medications to counteract the bone loss. Ask your doctor about this.

But what if you already have osteoporosis? Be assured that both physical and spiritual osteoporosis can be treated. Isaiah 58:11 promises, "And the LORD shall…make fat thy bones…." This refers to thin, osteoporotic bones that are made thicker (or fatter) by the Lord. Isaiah 66:14 also promises, "…your bones shall flourish like an herb…," which describes bones that are actively growing, building up instead of breaking down.

There are currently several types of medications to treat osteoporosis, including oral, injectable, intravenous, and intranasal. You should discuss with your doctor which one is best for you. In addition, the preventive measures that were discussed previously should be followed to maintain healthy bone structure.

If you have the misfortune to suffer an acute compression fracture of the spine, there is a surgical procedure called kyphoplasty that can help relieve pain and restore the height of the vertebra, keeping you from becoming bowed over. It consists of the use of a balloon device that is guided into proper position inside a collapsed vertebra with the aid of a fluoroscope. The surgeon then inflates the balloon to expand it and infuses a special bone cement into the area. Of course, all surgical procedures carry some risk, but this can be very effective. Jesus, by His Word, performed the first kyphoplasty two thousand years ago on the woman in Luke 13, discussed previously. God's Word is still able to heal today and give strength to our spiritual bones, enabling us to walk upright.

Physical osteoporosis, if untreated, can lead to total disability due to weakness, deformity, pain, and even the inability to walk or stand. Spiritual osteoporosis can be just as devastating, but it is equally treatable, for God has provided everything we need to be able to stand against Satan and not fall under times of stress.

We must first desire and partake of the sincere milk of the Word and apply it personally in order to grow spiritually. Then we must walk in that light. Through faith we understand and believe the important concept that we can stand on God's grace alone. Our strength does not lie in self-works, but in the power of the blood of Jesus, which atoned for our sins. If we are in Christ, and Christ is in us, then we have the same power to stand against Satan that Jesus did when He was tempted in the wilderness. We know in whom we stand, and we have no fear of falling, as stated by Jude in Jude 24–25: "Now unto him that is able to keep you from falling, and to present you faultless before the presence of his glory with exceeding joy; To the only wise God our Saviour, be glory and majesty, dominion and power, both now and ever. Amen."

SPIRITUAL ALZHEIMER'S

My topic in this chapter is "spiritual Alzheimer's disease." It is rated X—that is, for adults only, mature audiences. This is not for children or babes, because Alzheimer's is a disease that occurs in older people, as we age, and it is mostly characterized by forgetting. In the natural, as we progress from childhood to become mature adults, it is not unusual for us to begin to develop a little problem with memory, but that is not Alzheimer's disease. That is called the "benign senescence of aging." Sometimes it seems as though our "forgetter" is working overtime! Can anyone reading this relate to that?

In 1906 a German clinical psychiatrist named Alois Alzheimer described a case exhibiting a peculiar severe disease of the cerebral cortex involving memory and other behavioral disturbances. Other clinicians and physicians then began to discover similar cases in their practices. It was first called Alzheimer's disease in 1910, named after its discoverer. Now most people are familiar with it and perhaps have a friend or family member who is affected by it.

I am going to concentrate on the "forgetting" portion of this disease and apply it spiritually, for it is something that should characterize a mature Christian. God, the Ancient One, manifests this characteristic as described in Hebrews 10:17–18: "their sins and their iniquities will I remember no more" (v. 17), because "where remission of these is, there is no more offering for sin" (v. 18). The price has already been paid. God does not simply overlook sin, for when the debt has been paid in full, then it can be forgotten. The offering of the Lamb of God took away our sin; it has been erased.

It is much like the bill that you would receive if you saw me in my office. If you paid it completely, then you should not receive another bill. If you did, I would expect a call from you saying, "That has been paid, and I have proof of it." We should have the same attitude with our sin debt when Satan tries to tell us that our sins have not been covered, forgiven, and forgotten. We should tell him, "Well, I'm sorry, but you are wrong and I have proof. The account book, the Bible, states that the debt has been paid in full and my sins are remembered no more." God has paid for our sins. He purposely chose to forgive and to forget, and we should do the same.

Ephesians 4:31–32 instructs us: "Let all bitterness, and wrath, and anger, and clamor, and evil speaking, be put away from you, with all malice: And be ye kind one to another, tenderhearted, forgiving one another, even as God for Christ's sake hath forgiven you." If we are to forgive as God forgave, then that also includes the forgetting. He is our example. As we mature in the natural, the forgetting happens without trying. If we mature spiritually, it should also happen automatically. It is the nature of the new creation life in us to forgive and forget. As we grow up into "the stature of the fullness of Christ" (Eph. 4:13), we should have no more bitterness or anger toward a brother or sister or anyone. We forgive and forget through the Christ-life in us.

Speaking in the natural, from the standpoint of a physician, I will tell you that children *always* remember the bad things that you do to them. If you give them a shot, they will not forget it and will remember you the next time they see you and start crying. On the other hand, my elderly patients with Alzheimer's do not remember if you have ever done something painful to them. You can walk out of the room and come back in, and they will just smile at you as if nothing happened.

What about in the spiritual? God desires that we "grow up into him [Christ] in all things" (Eph. 4:15), "unto a perfect [mature, full-grown] man, unto the measure of the stature of the fullness of Christ" (Eph. 4:13), and be "no more children" (Eph. 4:14). As we grow up into Christ, maturing in Him, we will also forget the bad things that others have done to us in the past or the present. If we are unable to do this, then it means we are still children spiritually, needing to feed more upon the Word of His grace in order to finish growing up and to be conformed into His image.

The apostle Paul, a true mature saint, admits to developing spiritual Alzheimer's in his letter to the Philippians: "Brethren, I count not myself to have apprehended: but this one thing I do, *forgetting* those things which are behind…" (Phil. 3:13). He was saying that the one thing, the most important thing, was to forget everything in the past. This included all the good things as well as the bad. We are not to glory in our past accomplishments or live on our past blessings. After letting all those things go, forgetting them, refusing to live in them, then Paul says he could then reach forth unto those things that were ahead, and "press toward the mark for the prize of the high calling of God in Christ Jesus" (v. 14).

What about in the natural? What can we do if we start having trouble remembering things that are important? The best thing to do is to start writing them down. In fact, God does this for us spiritually, as stated in Hebrews 10:16: "This is the covenant that I will make with them after those days, saith the Lord, I will put my laws into their hearts, and in their minds will I write them." So, God gets out His little pen and He writes His Word inside of us, in our hearts and minds, and it becomes a part of us as we study it. The Word of God must go beyond a "mind thing," that is, a mental task of just trying to learn it, to memorize it. It needs to be written on the fleshly table of our hearts, inscribed with the pen of the Holy Spirit. God wrote the Ten Commandments on tablets of stone with His finger. Today He wants to write His Word on our hearts so that it literally becomes a part of us. I have had Alzheimer's patients who were not able to carry on a conversation and could not even recognize their own family, but they could quote Scripture. The Word of God was written on their heart and bypassed the brain.

Have you ever heard about someone tying a string around their finger to help them remember something? Maybe the idea originated from Proverbs 7:1 and 3: "My son, keep my words…" (v. 1), "bind them upon thy fingers, write them upon the table of thine heart" (v. 3). Proverbs 3:3 also instructs us to write the truth of God's Word upon our hearts: "Let not mercy and truth forsake thee [don't forget them]:…write them upon the table of thine heart."

Another thing that often happens with Alzheimer's patients is that they start talking to themselves (although we all do that a little). I always told patients that it is the only way to ensure a truly intelligent conversation! Would you be surprised to learn that the Scripture tells us that we are *supposed* to talk to ourselves? So perhaps when we do it, we are just trying to be more spiritual! Paul encourages Christians to do this in Ephesians 5:19: "Speaking to yourselves in psalms and hymns and spiritual songs, singing and making melody in your heart to the Lord." David also spoke to himself many times when he was discouraged, as in Psalm 42:11: "Why are thou cast down, O my soul? and why are thou disquieted within me? hope thou in God." And again in Psalm 103:1, he conversed with his soul: "Bless the LORD, O my soul: and all that is within me." So, go ahead and speak to yourself; it is scriptural and a sign of maturity.

As Alzheimer's disease progresses, patients reach a point where they forget where they are going or what they are doing. If they drive somewhere, they may not find their way home. If they walk out the door, they may get lost. They need someone to lead them in the right direction. It is no longer safe for them to be in the driver's seat. Likewise, as Christians, we should also progress to the stage where we hand over the keys to the Lord and let Him do the driving. We recognize that we really do need a Shepherd to guide us, and we cry out to the Lord as David did in Psalm 27:11: "Teach me thy way, O LORD, and lead me in a plain path." As children, we want to do it our way. Anyone who has been around children knows that a two-year-old will say, "No, *me* do it," when we try to show them how to do something. This is also true spiritually, but as we mature, we learn how to ask for God's direction and to yield to the Holy Spirit to teach us and guide us, instead of insisting on our own way.

Alzheimer's patients will eventually lose the capacity to make decisions, and therefore they need to choose a "power of attorney" who will do that for them when they are no longer able to do it for themselves. That person needs to be someone whom they trust completely, and they must have confidence that the person will make choices that are in their best interests. What about spiritually? We need to give God the power of attorney to choose for us, and say, "Lord, not my will, but Yours be done." Even Jesus did that in the Garden of Gethsemane when He prayed, "Nevertheless, not My will but Thine be done." He was willing to submit to His Father, leaving the choice to Him rather than to have His own way.

Romans 12:2 puts it this way: "And be not conformed to this world: but be ye transformed [changed] by the renewing [changing] of your mind." We need a new mind, so we must lose the old one. "Let this mind be in you, which was also in Christ Jesus" (Phil. 2:5). What mind was in Jesus? To let God choose for Him! When we do that, then we can do as David commanded in Psalm 37:5: "Commit thy way unto the LORD; trust also in him." Give Him your power of attorney. The aged apostle Paul had chosen God for his power of attorney for he told the young preacher Timothy, "I know whom I have believed, and am persuaded that he [God] is able to keep that which I have committed unto him" (2 Tim. 1:12). That is an example of complete trust: Everything in your life—your past, your present, and your future—are committed to Him. So why not give God your power of attorney and get out of the driver's seat, leaving all the decisions to Him, for He knows what is best.

One last thought concerning patients with Alzheimer's disease. If you were to visit a nursing home, you may be approached by a quaint little lady who asks, "Have you seen my mother? She said she would be here. I've been waiting for her. I know she's coming because she said she would." It seems as though they are constantly waiting for someone to come back.

Have you reached that stage of spiritual maturity, spiritual Alzheimer's, that you are eagerly waiting for Jesus to come back? We know according to the Scriptures that He is coming because He said He would. In John 14:2–3, Jesus said: "...I go to prepare a place for you. And if I go and prepare a place for you, I will come again, and receive you unto myself; that where I am, there ye may be also." When we put our trust in Him, we have nothing to worry about, and only one thing should occupy our minds: "Looking for that blessed hope, and the glorious appearing of the great God and our Saviour Jesus Christ" (Tit. 2:13).

A SPIRITUAL PANDEMIC

A pandemic is classified as a global outbreak of a disease and usually starts out locally as an epidemic and then spreads worldwide. Most viral pandemics have been caused by the influenza virus, which mutates in character from year to year. One of the deadliest ones was the Spanish flu of 1918, which killed between 20 to 50 million people. The swine flu (H1N1) was a new strain of that virus that killed approximately 700 million to 1.4 billion people worldwide. The regular seasonal influenza virus kills between 290 to 650 thousand per year. The coronavirus (COVID-19) was declared a pandemic on March 12, 2020, and its final devastation is yet to be determined.

When an infected person coughs or sneezes, the virus containing droplets are scattered out into the air as aerosol. The aerosol droplets land on objects close by, thus contaminating them, or they spread directly from person to person when they are in close proximity (within six feet) or by direct contact. Viruses can rapidly be spread in this manner if precautions are not taken.

Viruses are composed of genetic material (RNA or DNA) surrounded by a protein coat. They do not have the ability or cellular machinery to make proteins, and they cannot reproduce by themselves. They must invade a host cell and inject their own genetic material into it, which is then incorporated into the host cell's genetic material. It then causes the host cell to make the proteins necessary to reproduce itself. As a result, it multiplies rapidly. The new virus particles are subsequently released from that cell when it dies, and they quickly invade and take over other cells, doing the same thing over and over. Since a virus cannot reproduce itself unless it invades a host cell, it is important for an infected person to avoid close contact with other people. Without a host cell to replicate, the virus will die within a couple of weeks. The quarantining of infected persons has been utilized for hundreds of years to prevent the spread of diseases, even back in Bible days.

The Bible contains good information in the Old Testament regarding infectious diseases. The priests who ministered in the tabernacle in the wilderness were required to wash their hands in the brazen laver after offering sacrifices prior to entering the tabernacle. While this has an important spiritual application, it was also necessary physically. Anyone with a draining sore or a bloody issue was considered unclean and had to keep themselves separated from the rest of the people. More specifically, regarding an infectious disease, let us examine the regulations for leprosy, which was a major health concern in those days. Leviticus 13 describes how to diagnose an active case of leprosy. If a person met the criteria, he was considered "utterly unclean." Verse 45 tells us he was to put a covering upon his upper lip, which would be like a modern-day face mask. Verse 46 states, "...he is unclean: he shall dwell alone; without [outside] the camp shall his habitation be." In other words, he was to be quarantined, away from everyone else. This was, of course, to prevent the spread of that disease to other people.

Healthcare professionals are following similar guidelines today to limit the spreading of infectious diseases. Regarding the spread of COVID-19, they also restricted the gathering of large groups of people together to avoid personal contact as much as possible.

Now I would like to make a spiritual comparison of the spread of viruses to another important problem facing us today. The virus is like sin, which takes control over us and we are powerless in ourselves to stop it. Like the precautions recommended for limiting the spread of the COVID-19 virus, we are told by God to separate ourselves from sin: "Come out from among them, and be ye separate, saith the Lord, and touch not the unclean thing" (2 Cor. 6:17). God desires that as Christians we are to live a separated life and to avoid even the appearance of evil, but this is impossible in our own strength.

The sin virus infected man through Adam in the Garden of Eden. Since then it has been passed to all mankind and is a true pandemic. The sin virus has a 100 percent mortality rate, for "all have sinned, and come short of the glory of God" (Rom. 3:23), and the Law declares that "the soul that sinneth, it shall die." That does *not* leave anyone out, for we all have been infected. We have no power to fight off the sin virus, but God does. He provided a cure that is available for anyone who is willing to receive it. That cure is found in 1 Corinthians 15:22 and is 100 percent effective: "For as in Adam *all* die [we have all been infected], even so in Christ [if we accept him] shall *all* be made alive" (emphasis mine). What could be better than that?

No ventilator can breathe life into a soul that is dead, but the breath of life can be breathed into us by God as we are made alive through Christ. Have you accepted the cure? If not, why not? There is no shortage, for "where sin abounded, grace did much more abound" (Rom. 5:20). It is by God's grace that we are saved (given life) and the cure is injected into us in the person of Jesus Christ. When we accept Christ in our hearts, we are 100 percent protected from the deadly sin virus and given eternal life. "He that hath the Son hath life; and he that hath not the Son of God hath not life" (1 John 5:12).

If the previous guidelines are used in order to prevent the spread of something harmful, could we not also spread something that was good? In that case we would do the opposite. After Jesus' resurrection, just before He ascended back to heaven, He commanded His disciples, "Go ye into all the world, and preach the gospel to every creature" (Mark 16:15). They had become personally infected with the good news of the resurrection through close contact with Jesus Himself and now they were told to start spreading it around the world, infecting others. They were to do this by preaching, or spreading the gospel with their mouths, which contained the contagious droplets of the new Christianity virus.

Like any other pandemic, it started out locally as an epidemic and then became worldwide. We see this when Jesus told His followers in Acts 1:8, "...ye shall be witnesses unto me both in Jerusalem [locally], and in all Judea [regionally], and in Samaria, and unto the uttermost part of the earth [worldwide]." The pandemic of Christianity began initially with the twelve disciples and a few women, then increased to 120 who were gathered together in the upper room in

Jerusalem on the Day of Pentecost, when the Holy Spirit was poured out. But we also read that more than five hundred people had been in contact with Jesus at one time following His resurrection (1 Cor. 15:6). These also had the potential to become infected and spread the virus. However, the 120 in Jerusalem exposed an even bigger crowd of people, for we read in Acts 2 that a large multitude heard them speak and about three thousand of them became infected and believed. After that, "the Lord added to the church daily" (v. 47), those who were being saved, and the infection continued to spread by person-to-person contact.

A virus is spread by the droplets of water that come out of the mouth of an infected person. The aerosol droplets of those Christians were the Word of God and the gospel of Jesus Christ, which still has the power to infect anyone who is exposed to it, even today.

After the Day of Pentecost, we read in Acts 3 that Peter and John were going into the temple in Jerusalem to pray, and they met a lame beggar asking for money. Peter told him, "Silver and gold have I none; but such as I have give I thee: In the name of Jesus Christ of Nazareth rise up and walk" (Acts 3:6). What did Peter and John have? They had been infected with the Christianity virus, and as commanded by Jesus, they were spreading it through His name throughout Jerusalem to anyone with whom they had contact. Peter not only spread the virus by what came out of his mouth, but he reached out and took the lame man by the hand, making direct physical contact. This promptly spread the infection to him, and he was immediately healed and began to walk and leap and praise God, which in turn infected others around him.

The religious leaders of that day now recognized the seriousness of the epidemic of Christianity, and they tried desperately to keep it from becoming a pandemic. They took Peter and John aside after that incident to question them. The chief priests and rulers feared that it would keep spreading and quickly held a council among themselves saying, "But that it spread no further among the people, let us straightly threaten them, that they speak henceforth to no man in this name" (Acts 4:17), "…and commanded them not to speak at all nor teach in the name of Jesus" (v. 18). Basically, they were telling Peter and John to cover their mouths with a "mask" of silence, much like we put a mask on an infected person to limit the spread of infected aerosol droplets. However, Peter and John refused to do this and replied, "We cannot but speak the things which we have seen and heard" (v. 20). They could not hold back the breath of the Holy Spirit, which was now flowing through them: "…for out of the abundance of the heart the mouth speaketh" (Matt. 12:34).

Since then, Christianity has become a pandemic through the name of Jesus. Many have tried over the years to stamp it out, and Satan continues to do this today. He persists in trying to remove the name of Jesus or the symbol of the cross from schools, government offices, places of work, and even our homes. Christians all over the world are being persecuted, tortured, and killed in an effort to eradicate the name of Jesus and Christianity.

Sadly, there are many in America who claim to be Christians who have never really been infected. They have no symptoms of the virus that are detectable in their lives.

What symptoms would be expected to be manifested? The three most important symptoms that confirm a suspected case of Christianity would be praise, joy, and love. Praise and joy would be likely to be manifested in spite of dire circumstances. We find evidence of this in Acts 5, which states that the apostles, after being beaten for preaching in the name of Jesus, were "rejoicing that they were counted worthy to suffer shame for his name" (v. 41). We find further evidence of these symptoms in Paul and Silas after they were beaten and thrown into the inner prison for preaching and had their feet placed in the stocks. At midnight they "prayed, and sang praises unto God…" (Acts 16:25). Perhaps they were delirious with the fever from the infection! Jesus Himself confirmed that love was an important criterion in the diagnosis, as stated in John 13:35: "By this shall all men know that ye are my disciples, if ye have love one to another."

A person cannot become a Christian simply by hearing about Jesus and reading about Him or memorizing the Bible any more than a person can become infected with the coronavirus simply by hearing about it on the news or reading about it on the internet. We must have personal contact with Jesus by letting the gospel touch our hearts and infect our souls. In order to claim the name of Jesus and become a Christian, we must have had close enough contact with Him to be able to say with John, "we have looked upon, and our hands have *handled*, of the Word of life" (1 John 1:1, emphasis mine). John was so close to Jesus that he leaned on Jesus' breast and was called the "disciple whom Jesus loved." The Word of life was Jesus Himself.

As a result of such close personal contact, we become infected, and there will be evidence in our lives that others can see. With Christ in our lives, we can then touch others, spread His love, and continue to preach the gospel with our lives, as well as with our mouths.

SPIRITUAL HEART TRANSPLANT

Do you want a new heart? If you are born again, you have a new heart. But how did you get that new heart, and why did you need it?

In Ezekiel 36:26, God offers Israel a new heart, a spiritual heart transplant. "A new heart will I give you and a new spirit will I put within you: and I will take away the stony heart out of your flesh, and I will give you an heart of flesh." Israel's heart had become hardened and turned to stone and away from God. The Israelites had spiritual heart failure.

I am going to compare this spiritual heart transplant to a physical heart transplant. Organ transplantation is one of the modern miracles of medicine that allows some people to have a continued life that they wouldn't have had otherwise. You must keep in mind that in order for a heart transplant to take place, a donor with a healthy heart must die. Therefore, the gift of a transplant is a true gift of life; likewise it is in the spiritual realm.

I am truly amazed at the medical accuracy of the Bible. When a person receives a heart transplant, it is because their old heart has become so diseased and weak for various reasons that medications or further surgical intervention will no longer benefit. In physical end-stage heart failure, the tissue of the heart becomes fibrosed or hardened such that it is no longer able to pump effectively. The book of Ezekiel accurately describes this as a "stony" heart.

What is end-stage heart failure? In end-stage heart failure, the heart is no longer able to keep up with the workload necessary to pump the blood to all the other organs and tissues of the body. Consequently, fluid backs up into the lungs, resulting in congestion., hence the term "congestive heart failure," or "CHF." In early heart failure, this can be controlled with medications and special pacemakers, but if it progresses, these may no longer be effective.

What about in the spiritual? In Matthew 11:28, Jesus invited all who labored and were heavy laden to come unto Him and He would give them rest. If we are working under the burden of the law and are not able to keep up with that workload, we will go into spiritual heart failure. We cannot do it; we cannot hold up under the heavy burden of the law. We find ourselves under the sentence of death, since the law says, "The soul that sinneth it shall die" (Ezek. 18:4). This includes all mankind, for Romans 3:23 declares, "For all have sinned, and come short of the glory of God." Our hearts have failed! We are in end-stage heart failure and in need of a new heart, the heart of Jesus, so that we may rest in the finished work of Calvary.

In the physical, the criteria to be eligible for a heart transplant is that your heart is so weak that you would be expected to die within six months without it. In other words you must have a diagnosis of impending death. Likewise, in the spiritual you must recognize your hopeless condition and be willing to accept a new heart.

God has evaluated man's heart and found it to be incurably diseased in Jeremiah 17:9–10: "The heart is deceitful above all things, and desperately wicked [you have a bad heart]: who can know it? I the LORD search the heart, I try the reins."

Only God, the true Heart Specialist, can know the heart. If you have a bad heart, you go to a doctor who is a specialist to see if anything more can be done. You recognize your need and you go to the one who can meet that need. Through a series of tests, the doctor is able to come up with the diagnosis and can then offer you a heart transplant. God has already done this for us and is able to meet our need. All we have to do is to say, "Yes."

Again, concerning the medical accuracy of the Bible, Jeremiah 17:10 says, "I the LORD search the heart, I try the reins." Do you know what the "reins" are? They are the kidneys! We get the term *renal* from this same root word. The kidneys were used in that day to describe the inner parts of our being, similar to the way in which we use the word *heart* today. It is no accident that God chose to use the kidney in conjunction with the heart instead of the liver or the bowel, for there is a direct medical association between the two organs. In the natural if a person is being evaluated for a heart transplant, the kidneys must be evaluated also. The first major organ, besides the brain, that the heart pumps blood to is the kidneys. As heart failure progresses, the kidneys also begin to fail due to decreased blood flow. It is possible that you may also need a kidney transplant, as you must have adequate kidney function for a heart transplant. God was fully aware of that when He wrote the Book; it was not coincidental. This was written long before medical textbooks were ever written!

God knows every little part of us. He knows our hearts better than we do. Our hearts are "desperately wicked and deceitful above all things." No matter how good a person we try to be or how much love we try to show, if we are doing it through our own ability, sooner or later we will break under the load. The anger will come out, and we will get tired of doing good works and we will fail. The Scripture says, "Be not weary in well doing," but we are going to get weary if we are trying to do it out of the goodness of our own heart, for there is no goodness in our own heart. We *all* have heart failure because we cannot do the good things that we want to do. "There is none that doeth good, no, not one" (Rom. 3:12). This is also true physically, for a person with end-stage heart failure has reached the point that they are unable to do any type of work. They even have trouble performing their normal activities of daily living or any of the things they want to do.

The apostle Paul acknowledged that in Romans 7:18–19 when he discovered that in his flesh, he was not able to do the good that he wanted to do. In desperation, he cried out in verse 24: "Who shall deliver me from the body of this death?" He recognized that the old creation heart was not able to please God, so he went to the Heart Specialist to "try his heart and reins." He knew he was under the sentence of death, as in 2 Corinthians 1:9: "But we had the sentence of death in ourselves, that we should not trust in ourselves, but in God which raiseth the dead." It takes a new creation heart to please God. This same problem applies to all of us. Paul's physical life was in danger, but spiritually none of us would escape death from spiritual heart failure, apart from Christ.

The wickedness of our heart has nothing to do with our upbringing or whether or not we were raised in a Christian home. It simply has to do with the fact that we are all sinners.

This isn't intended to be a sermon about salvation or how to get saved. It is a message about how great the gift of God was to us. Sometimes we fail to recognize the magnitude of that gift of life and how great was His grace toward us.

In Ezekiel 18:31, God again admonishes Israel to accept His offer of life: "Cast away from you all your transgressions, whereby ye have transgressed; and make you a new heart and a new spirit: for why will ye die, O house of Israel?" The Doctor is telling Israel, "You have a bad heart, and you are going to die; but I'm offering you a new heart. Why will you die? All you need to do is take My new heart." Likewise, we have the same terminal diagnosis, so why will *we* die?

Now, let us assume that you have been evaluated for a heart transplant and placed on a waiting list. What does it mean to be on a waiting list? It means that you are waiting around for someone who is going to be your donor, who matches you, to die. Think about that! You are waiting for someone to die in order that you may live.

Before you can receive a new heart, a donor must die at the right place and the right time. In Galatians 4:4–5, we read that "when the fullness of time was come, God sent forth his Son made of a woman, made under the law, to redeem them that were under the law." So, when the fullness of time had come, the *exact right time* that God had planned, He sent His Son. What was the purpose of sending His Son? To die! For God so loved the world that He sent His Son to die for us.

The person who is put on a transplant list must carry a pager or a phone and be waiting for the call. When they hear the call that a donor has been found, they must be ready to go immediately. They can't say, "I have something I need to do first; I just can't come today." The donor must die at the right time and place that enables the recipient of the heart to reach that location within a very short period of time; he must go immediately or it will be too late for the transplant to be performed. This is also true spiritually; it has to be *now*. When we hear the call, we must go. God had it all planned out, when to send His Son and when to call us. How do we receive the call? Through the Word. We hear His voice, and we must be willing and ready to go. Just as Rebecca, in the Old Testament, we must be willing to say, "Yes, I will go." We can't wait until tomorrow. He may come today. Now is the time to receive your new heart. Second Corinthians 6:2 tells us, "...*now* is the accepted time; behold, now is the day of salvation."

Who is capable of being your donor? A donor must match, as closely as possible, the recipient's size, and the donor must be of the right tissue and blood type. It is not possible to take an adult's heart and transplant it into an infant. Do you understand the correlation? In the natural it must fit and be compatible. Since *we* cannot change, our donor must match us. We cannot make ourselves match the donor. Jesus had to match us. God's Son had to be born of a woman, to become like us. God could not put His heart in us; God's heart would not fit.

We cannot be like God. That was one of the lies of Satan in the Garden of Eden. He asked Eve, "What did God say?"

She replied that she would die if she ate of or touched that tree. Satan deceived her by saying, "No, you won't die; you will become like God."

No, we can't be like God; we can't have God's heart, because the donor doesn't match! He is the wrong tissue type. John 1:1 says, "In the beginning was the Word, and the Word was with God, and the Word was God." And in verse 14: "The Word became flesh, and dwelt among us." The Son of God became the Son of Man, and so the tissue type now matches!

We could not become like God, so He became like us. Jesus said in John 10:11: "I am the good shepherd: the good shepherd giveth his life for the sheep." The donor had to die to give us life. If we are going to become His sheep, we need a lamb's heart. It has to be a match; it must be the same tissue type. The Word of God became the Good Shepherd, but also the Lamb of God (John 1:29). The Good Shepherd became the Lamb and was slain so that we could have His heart.

The blood type also had to match. Jesus had to take on a body of flesh and blood to give us a new heart that was compatible. In Hebrews 7:26, we see that He was not only the sacrifice (the Lamb), but He was also our High Priest: "For such a high priest became us." He became a man, not only to have flesh and blood, but to be touched by the feeling of our infirmities. He became the perfect donor for us. He was now our blood type and tissue type, and He willingly gave His life for us.

The gift of a transplant should never be taken lightly in the natural or the spiritual, for it requires the death of the donor. It is an incredible gift of love and life. We often quote

John 3:16 without fully recognizing the value of that life that was given for us and what He went through when He left His throne in glory to become a man, to become like us. He took upon Himself the form of sinful man, and He who knew no sin became sin for us. We can't even begin to comprehend the emotional and physical suffering that He endured in order to give us a new heart. He looked beyond the suffering of the cross to the joy that was set before Him, the joy of reigning with His bride.

In Psalm 51:10, David pleaded, "Create in me a clean heart, O God." A donor heart must be "clean," free of blocked vessels. In the natural, the arteries are examined to be sure they are clean. And the size and weight of the heart is checked to see if it is appropriate and that it is not enlarged, hardened, or fibrosed. The heart must be healthy with good blood flow. It is also true in the spiritual. Jesus' heart was clean and pure; He was without sin. The Lamb of God was without blemish or spot, perfect, with a perfect heart.

When we accept this heart, we become a lamb with the Lamb's heart, a heart that desires to do the Father's will. This is the same heart that said, "Not My will, but Thine be done"; the same heart that cried, "Father, forgive them." It is that kind of love that is shed abroad in our hearts by the Holy Ghost, because we now have a new, clean heart. We have the free flow of the blood of the Lamb of God in us to manifest the life of Christ. We cannot with the old creation heart have that kind of love. It is only possible with a new heart. Works could not earn a new heart, but after we receive the new heart, we are able to perform work. Our works will then be His works, for it is Christ in us.

So, as God asked Israel, "Why will ye die?" Why not agree with the Great Physician's diagnosis of heart failure and impending death and submit to the scalpel of God's Word and receive the gift of life: His new heart? The Donor is waiting; *now* is the accepted time. The Holy Spirit is calling. Can you hear the call? God has a call on your life. He wants you to have His heart to do His will. Will you say, "Yes"? And when you awake from surgery after your transplant, this will be your testimony: "My heart is fixed, O God, my heart is fixed: I will sing and give praise" (Ps. 57:7).

ABOUT THE AUTHOR

Dr. Victoria Moots grew up in rural Kansas and practiced general/family medicine in the small town of Kingman for thirty-two years before retiring in 2019. She was the first female doctor in that area. Her practice included everything from delivering babies to seeing patients in the clinic, the hospital, the nursing homes, and the emergency room. In addition, she served as county coroner, county health officer, the medical director of emergency medical services, and the medical director of four area nursing homes.

Upon graduation from high school, she attended Grace & Glory Bible School in Kansas City, Missouri, as she felt the call of God on her life. After completion of that program, she married Larry, her husband, and they moved back to Kansas. For a period of time, they operated the House of Refuge rescue mission in Hutchinson. She was also a volunteer for the crisis hotline as well as a chaplain for female prisoners. By this time they had four children, but when their youngest was only two years old, Larry was injured in a fall and unable to work for a while. As a result, Victoria, better known as Vicky, had to enter the workforce as a nurse's aide in a nursing home. That job inspired her to further her education and to enter the medical field. Ever since childhood, she had wanted to be a doctor, but she had never had the finances to pursue that dream. However, now she discovered that she was eligible for financial assistance and scholarships. So, with four children, at the age of thirty-one, she started college as a premed student. She received her DO degree from Texas College of Osteopathic Medicine in Ft. Worth, Texas, in 1986, becoming the first female in that school to graduate as valedictorian.

The family then returned to Hutchinson, Kansas, while she completed her general internship at Riverside Hospital in Wichita. In 1987 she entered medical practice with Dr. Lester Donley at the Donley Clinic in Kingman, purchasing the clinic after his retirement. Dr. Moots is affectionately known by many of her longtime patients as "Dr. Vicky."

Besides being a physician, she is a minister and volunteer pastor of the Lerado Country Church, and she has donated her services for medical mission trips through Medical Ministry International.

Dr. Moots and her husband, Larry, have four children and seven grandchildren, and they were married over fifty years prior to his death in 2019.

If you have questions or are interested in having me come to speak contact me at: doctorvmoots@gmail.com or call 620 532-1407.

CPSIA information can be obtained
at www.ICGtesting.com
Printed in the USA
BVHW041030181120
593417BV00017B/645